T0226290

Lecture Notes in Computer Science

Lecture Notes in Computer Science

Edited by G. Goos and J. Hartmanis

290

Tung X. Bui

Co-oP

A Group Decision Support System for
Cooperative Multiple Criteria Group Decision Making

Springer-Verlag

Berlin Heidelberg New York London Paris Tokyo

Editorial Board

D. Barstow W. Brauer P. Brinch Hansen D. Gries D. Luckham
C. Moler A. Pnueli G. Seegmüller J. Stoer N. Wirth

Author

Tung X. Bui
Institute for Automation and Operations Research
University of Fribourg, Miséricorde
CH-1700 Fribourg, Switzerland

and

Department of Administrative Sciences
Naval Postgraduate School
Monterey, CA 93943, USA

CR Subject Classification (1987): H.4, H.1, C.2, C.5

ISBN 3-540-18753-7 Springer-Verlag Berlin Heidelberg New York
ISBN 0-387-18753-7 Springer-Verlag New York Berlin Heidelberg

This work is subject to copyright. All rights are reserved, whether the whole or part of the material is concerned, specifically the rights of translation, reprinting, re-use of illustrations, recitation, broadcasting, reproduction on microfilms or in other ways, and storage in data banks. Duplication of this publication or parts thereof is only permitted under the provisions of the German Copyright Law of September 9, 1965, in its version of June 24, 1985, and a copyright fee must always be paid. Violations fall under the prosecution act of the German Copyright Law.

© Springer-Verlag Berlin Heidelberg 1987
Printed in Germany

ACKNOWLEDGMENTS

This research could not have been achieved without the help, encouragement, and support of many people. I am grateful to Professor Matthias Jarke (University of Passau). His continued assistance and constant support aided appreciably in strengthening both the content and presentation of this work. I am indebted to Professor Edward Stohr (New York University) who offered careful and constructive guidelines for building an integrated decision support system interface for multiple criteria decision methods. I am also grateful to Professor Melvin F. Shakun (New York University) who gave me invaluable advice throughout the exploration of various techniques of aggregation of preferences. I am obligated to Professors Michael Ginzberg (Case Western Reserve University), Paul Gray (Claremont Graduate School), Eric Jacquet-Lagreze (University of Paris, Dauphine), Benn Konsynski (Harvard University), Henry Lucas Jr. (New York University) and Jacques Pasquier (University of Fribourg). All of them participated much with unstinted cooperation. Also, I would like to thank my colleagues at the US Naval Postgraduate School. Professors James Suchan and Dan Dolk contributed in the building of the contingency model for GDSS use discussed in Chapter 9. Professors Nancy Roberts, Taracad Sivasankaran and James Suchan, as well as my former officer students, Young Fiyol, Amy Hughes, Dan Webb and Mary Woodberry participated in the evaluation and testing of Co-oP. Christos Skindilias initiated the second version of Co-oP. Kurt Egbert, Andy Kardos, Mike Neely, and Bob Wooldridge deserve special credits in maintaining Co-oP and developing TOUCHSTONE, a Co-oP front-end for group generation of alternatives and evaluation criteria. Special thanks to Chris Perry who helped edit this book.

Finally, I must express my gratitude to the Swiss National Foundation for Scientific Research for its indispensable support for this research. Also, support from the Naval Postgraduate School Research Foundation permitted the empirical study on Co-oP use. Without these supports, it would have been impossible to have accomplished this work.

Tung X. Bui
The US Naval Postgraduate School
Monterey, California and
University of Fribourg, Switzerland

PREFACE

Decision Support Systems (DSS) — introduced as a concept in the early 1970's — are computerized systems intended to assist managers in preparing and/or justifying decisions. In recent years, especially with the proliferation of microcomputers, DSS usage has enjoyed considerable growth, due to their elegant integration of databases, decision models (e.g., spreadsheets, statistical models, optimization models), and user interfaces (e.g., menu, mouse, windowing). Traditionally, DSS have been single-user systems although it is well-known that many relevant decisions are made or at least prepared by groups rather than individuals. At the same time, progress in communication technologies enforces faster and faster decisions, thus making face-to-face meetings by such groups more and more difficult.

This book presents an early attempt to integrate DSS methods with computer-assisted group techniques and micro-based communication technology. It has two objectives. First, it provides a general understanding of distributed group decision making and its requirements with respect to computerized support. Second, it presents the design of a specific group decision support system, Co-oP, characterized by the following design characteristics:

(1) The decision setting is *cooperative* as contrasted to hostile. Although negotiations take place, there is no consideration of intentional misrepresentation of data or preferences.

(2) Decisions are made in a *distributed and democratic* fashion. Each decision maker has his own workstation (personal computer) connected to others via a network. There is no group leader but only a chauffeur or secretary to expedite the discussion. The arbitration among different opinions (aggregation of preferences

and negotiation support) is provided by the system itself rather than by a human. Norms for the group decision process are agreed upon by the group but enforced by the system automatically, although mechanisms are provided for changing the rules of discussion dynamically.

(3) *Multiple Criteria Decision Methods* (MCDM) form the kernel of the system and the basis for exchange of information among the decision makers. This together with game-theoretic axioms, provides a formal basis for the otherwise very unclear tasks of group decision support. However, group decision making is not pressed into a static formal framework. Rather, the MCDM approach is embedded into a process-oriented group decision methodology that also includes the use of more informal group techniques, ranging from Delphi and Nominal Group Techniques to simple electronic mail and computer conferencing.

The approach in this book integrates theoretical work on extending computerized decision methods from the single-user to the multiple-user case. The book outlines a design framework for developing a generalized architecture for GDSS that emphasizes structured man-machine-man communication. It also discusses initial results of an empirical evaluation of a Pascal-based prototype implemented on a network of microcomputers. The experiences reported in this book seem to confirm the opinion that the development of group decision support systems is an important area in Information Systems research that deserves much further study by computer scientists.

Matthias Jarke
University of Passau
Passau, West Germany

CONTENTS

1. INTRODUCTION

This book focuses on multiple criteria group decision support systems. In particular, it analyzes, designs, implements and evaluates a Decision Support System for Cooperative Multiple Criteria Group Decision-Making (Co-oP). This introductory chapter discusses the purposes and significance of the proposed research, outlines its scope, limitations and anticipated contributions, and presents its organization.

1.1 PURPOSES AND SIGNIFICANCE OF THE STUDY

The objectives of this research are twofold:

1.   To develop a framework for designing a distributed computer-based DSS framework to support group problem solving. It is easily observed that the responsibility for making a decision often belongs to a group of individuals rather than to a single person. In such cases, the group must choose a method for finding a consensus leading to a 'best' solution or compromise.

    From a Decision Support System viewpoint, despite the existence of extensive and interdisciplinary literature related to group decision-making (see Chapter 3), it remains extremely difficult to implement theoretical analyses for practical applications.

2.   To elaborate theoretical and methodological foundations for performing multiple levels of integration of multiple criteria group

DSS; in particular to integrate different Multiple Criteria Decision Methods (MCDM), to integrate MCDM with other decision models and computer based communication techniques, and to discuss the structure of a Knowledge-based Model Management System for coordinating MCDM and supporting models.

Recent work on Multiple Criteria Decision Methods (MCDM) have shown that MCDM have proven useful in supporting decision-making (see section 2.1). Due to their capability to allow consideration of multiple conflicting objectives and of the decision maker's subjective evaluation, MCDM algorithms could be systematically combined and used as a vehicle – as opposed to a stand-alone decision model – to integrate various approaches to group problem solving.

The rationale of such an integration is fourfold:

1. To generate a synergistic effect that could not be achieved in separate or specific MCDM and other group decision tools. In other words, the implementation and use of such an integrated DSS would result in greater effectiveness than the sum of the effectiveness provided by separate use of techniques that are designed to resolve only one of the multiple problems found in group decision-making. For example, sequential use of multiple MCDM to resolve a multiple criteria problem can reduce the number of information searches, and hence the costs of searches, significantly as compared to the use of a single non-integrated MCDM (see section 5.3.2).

2. To support division of decision tasks according to the distribution of organizational power (either formal or informal) among decision makers (see section 5.3.3 and Chapter 12).

3. To implement a prototype that demonstrates the feasibility of the design strategies advocated in this research (see Chapter 8). Such a prototype can be used as an experimental tool to evaluate the effectiveness of group DSS in supporting group decision-making (see Chapters 9 and 10).

4. To outline a framework for analyzing and designing a purposeful and evolutionary Knowledge-based Model Management System to control coordination of integrated decision models, and assure a user-oriented, situation-dependent and circumstance-shaped DSS in an organizational context (see Chapters 11 and 12).

The significance of this research is highlighted by the development of an interdisciplinary and integrated framework for supporting collective decision-making, and by the implementation of a usable tool that can be effectively applied to a wide range of collective decision problems.

The implementation of Co-oP has also permitted empirical research to assess the performance, effectiveness and impact of Group Decision Support Systems on organizations (see Chapter 9).

1.2 SCOPE, LIMITATIONS AND ANTICIPATED CONTRIBUTIONS

Bearing in mind that the group decision-making problem is substantially more difficult than the single person decision problem, some limitations on the scope of research are necessary:

1. This research primarily focuses on the group problem solving in a cooperative environment in which decision makers interact in a friendly and trusting manner. It also concentrates on the

organizational decision situation in which the decision makers share the same set of problems and attempt to reach a common solution. This excludes another frequent collective decision situation in which each party has an individual set of decision outcomes often found, for example, in international negotiations (e.g., Barclay and Peterson, 1976). However, modification of the GDSS functional requirements to support non-cooperation is deliberated in Chapter 11.

2. This research also concentrates on the Model and Communications components of DSS for multiple criteria group decision-making. Issues related to the Dialogue and Data components will only be raised as they interact with the two other components, but will not be discussed and treated in detail.

3. From a system development life-cycle point of view, the proposed work provides only limited evaluation. Due to the inherent complexity of empirical research in collective decision-making, only the effectiveness of centralized and distributed GDSS is experimentally tested. It is expected, however, that the early findings reported in this work will lead to future large-scale experimental studies.

This research anticipates the following contributions:

1. **Theoretical and methodological contributions:**

First, in the Decision Support Systems (DSS) discipline, this work elaborates a general framework to design a distributed computer-based DSS framework for group decision-making which is – with a few exceptions (see section 3.3.1) – currently missing in the literature.

Second, in the Multiple Criteria Decision-Making (MCDM) discipline, this research contributes to current efforts of the MCDM research community to develop iterative algorithms and interactive DSS techniques to help improve assessment of group preferences and their consistency. Furthermore, this work proposes a contingency approach to multiple criteria group problem solving methods necessary for merging multiple criteria decision models with problem solving heuristics.

Third, this research investigates design issues to embed decision support capabilities into Office Information Systems (OIS) that so far have been preoccupied with automating clerical office functions.

2.   **Practical contributions**:

An effective single user DSS should support unstructured decision situations, and enhance the cognitive decision-making process (Ginzberg and Stohr, 1982). In addition to these advantages, the DSS for cooperative group decision-making (Co-oP) designed in this study is expected to provide the following capabilities: (i) to serve geographically dispersed users, (ii) to allow time to mediate discussion topics by providing sequential and/or online group decision-making, (iii) to assist all phases of the group decision-making process from the problem definition phase to the consensus seeking phase, (iv) to enhance equality of participation in group discussion by offering the same decision support to each user, (vi) and to facilitate technical information exchange by promoting written communication.

1.3 ORGANIZATION OF THE BOOK

This research consists of thirteen chapters. Chapter 2 defines basic terms and describes the context of the study. Chapter 3 reviews the interdisciplinary literature on group and multiple criteria group problem solving from a DSS engineering perspective. The roles and functions of group DSS are discussed in chapter 4. Chapter 5 explores requirements analyses and design issues of the model component of multiple criteria group decision support systems (MC-GDSS). Chapter 6 issues guidelines for designing the MC-GDSS dialogue component. Chapter 7 outlines communications requirements and protocols in group DSS. It particularly advocates the integration of a communications component in DSS for group problem solving.

The systems architecture and the software components of Co-oP, a multiple criteria DSS for cooperative group decision-making is described in Chapter 8. Chapter 9 examines GDSS applicability from an organizational perspective. A contingency model of GDSS used is discussed. Some elements of the model were empirically tested using two different GDSS settings: 'decision room' and distributed in Chapter 10. Chapter 11 reflects the problem of non-cooperation in GDSS. Some solutions are advanced to partially tackle competitiveness in collective decision-making. Chapter 12 expands the design of Co-oP into the general context of organizational decision-making process. Summary of results and suggestions for future research are discussed in Chapter 13.

2. DEFINITION OF TERMS AND CONTEXT OF THE DESIGN STUDY

This chapter provides basic definitions and concepts necessary for understanding the analysis and design of multiple criteria group decision support systems. It also delimits the boundaries of the proposed study.

2.1 MULTIPLE CRITERIA DECISION METHODS

2.1.1 Definitions and Concepts

Multiple criteria decision methods (MCDM) can be best defined by contrasting them with traditional decision models:

1. MCDM allow analyses of several criteria simultaneously or concurrently. (The terms criteria, goals, attributes, objectives are interchangeably used in the MCDM literature to identify references for evaluation). These criteria may be either quantifiable (cost, weight, etc.) or non-quantifiable (quality of service, aesthetics, etc.). More importantly, at least from the decision maker's viewpoint, the objectives often work against each other: the improvement or achievement of one criterion can be accomplished only at the expense of another. The location of a production plant may be best used to illustrate the nature of conflicting objectives often encountered in decision-making. A production plant near a business center would be convenient for sales but could be costly and limited in space. Conversely, a production plant in a remote area would largely satisfy the expendability criterion but also

would lead to high cost of transportation. Similarly, choosing a computer system, prioritizing projects, managing a waste disposal network are among numerous situations in which interests are multiple and contradictory.

2.   MCDM also allow consideration of the decision makers' subjective evaluation which is often crucial in decision problems. In most MCDM, the decision maker can express his preferences by weighing the evaluation criteria, making pairwise judgments or by simply giving an ordinal ranking of a set or subset of alternatives.

From this perspective, MCDM, by means of more or less formalized models, attempt to:

1.   Help the decision maker(s) to assess objectives that might intervene in the decision-making process, and,

2.   Improve the coherence between the evolution of the decision-making process and the changes in the user(s)' preferences.

Experience with MCDM has shown that when the decision maker assesses criteria, weighs their relative importance, and evaluates alternatives according to the selected criteria, he often discovers preferences that he was not aware of, and becomes able to structure problems that previously had not been clearly stated (Zeleny, 1982). It is generally acknowledged that the greater the correspondence between the results suggested by an analytical tool and the decision maker's intuitive judgments, the higher the level of confidence. In fact, the decision maker's confidence that a 'best' solution has been reached is the ultimate objective of MCDM, regardless of whether this decision is optimal or satisfying.

Thus, the use of MCDM is particularly relevant when a decision maker faces a hard choice among alternatives in which none of them stands out from the others as clearly the best choice: each alternative is good in some criteria but less good in some others. Selection of candidates for a business school (Moscarola and Roy, 1977), portfolio selection and bonds ranking (Nguyen, 1981), plant location (Lochard and Siskos, 1981), and selection of computer systems (Bui and Pasquier, 1984) are some of the problems that have been successfully treated by MCDM.

2.1.2   The MCDM Input-Process-Output Paradigm

Figure 2.1 describes the general process of MCDM, by referring to the traditional Input-Tool-Output relation (Bui, 1984).

1.   **The Input component** : The Input dimension includes two important components, a set of coherent alternatives and the decision maker(s)' preferences.

The *alternatives* are the possible, relevant and efficient courses of actions given a particular decision problem. In MCDM, actions are explicitly assumed 'naturally' mutually exclusive. If this is not the case, one might have to 'artificially' segment them into mutually exclusive subsets of independent, fragmented actions. The decision makers' *preferences* must be clearly defined in some models whereas they can be less specified in others (specified versus fuzzy evaluation). Preferences can also be fixed and very precise or variable and unknown throughout the decision process (deterministic versus stochastic evaluation). Finally, preferences

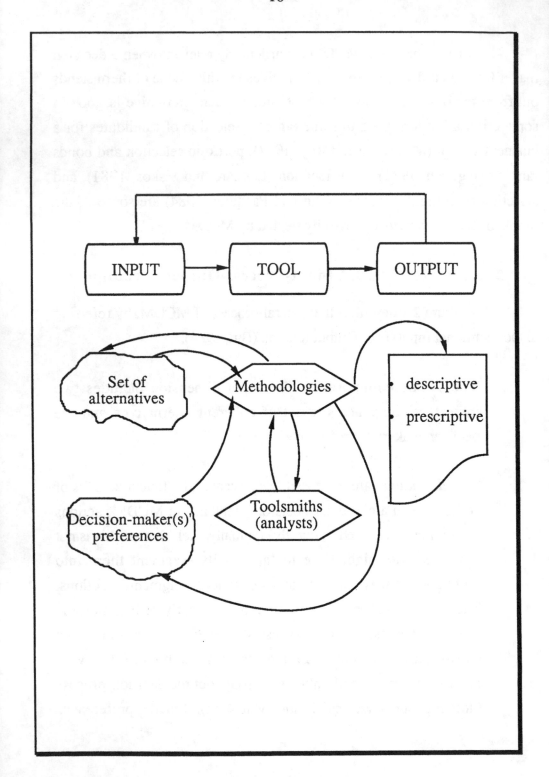

Figure 2.1. The Input-Tool-Relation in MCDM

may have a local structure or a global structure (disaggregation or aggregation of preferences).

2. **The Tool component** : The tools are made up by the methodology used and the analyst(s) required(s) for MCDM. The purpose of the tool is to help assess the decision maker's preferences based on the expected preferences of the courses of actions, and to search for a solution or compromise. The underlined methodology can be algorithmically precise (for example, multiobjective linear programming) or heuristic (for example, spatial proximity). Quantitative techniques such as simulation models can also be used as preliminary analyses prior to the use of a MCDM. The analyst(s) can be the decision maker, the MCDM expert or a MCDM computerized decision support system. The human expert often plays the role of intermediary between the user and the model. The degree of participation of the intermediary varies according to the methodology adopted. In some MCDM, a specialist is indispensable. In some others, the end-user can interact more or less directly with the model.

3. **The Output component** : The *output* or results presented by a MCDM to the user can be descriptive (for example, scenario methods) or prescriptive (for example, utility models). Unlike conventional econometric or OR methods that often overwhelm the user by a huge amount of information, MCDM often provide a short synthetic analysis of a decision and its consequences. Ranks, zero-one matrices and graphs are common outputs in MCDM to indicate the selected alternatives, often called the decision outcome.

4. **The arrows**: The arrows reflect the process-oriented approach of
    multiple criteria decision-making. As opposed to the outcome-
    oriented approach, the *process-oriented approach* focuses on
    understanding the decision process. Once one understands the
    process of decision-making, one can predict the outcome. This
    explains the descriptive-to-prescriptive relation in the Output
    component.

2.2 DECISION SUPPORT SYSTEMS

2.2.1   Definitions and Concepts

DSS may be defined as a computer-based problem solving
method that attempts to support decision makers to deal with unstructured,
ill-structured or under-specified problems. Table 2.1 relates the evolution
of key concepts found in DSS definitions.

A DSS is often viewed as being composed of three main
components: the Dialogue component, the Model component and the Data
component (Figure 2.2).

The *Dialogue component* consists of three main units: The user
interface unit provides the links between the user and the system.
Conventional man-machine interaction often has a menu-driven style and a
hard copy output. Recent technology continues to enhance the man-
machine interaction by using color graphics, sounds, mouses, joysticks,
speech synthesizer etc. The second unit of the Dialogue component is the
inter-module linkage unit which provides the liaisons with the Model
component and the Data component. Finally, the responsibility of the third
unit is to guarantee smooth operation of the Dialogue component.

The two most important units of the *Model component* are the
Model Base Management and the Model Execution. The role of the Model

John Little (1970)
Decision Calculus -- A Model-base set of procedures of processing
data and judgments to *assist* a manager in his decision making.

Gorry and Scott-Morton (1971)
Systems to support managerial decision makers in *unstructured* or
semi-unstructured situations.

Peter Keen (1978)
DSS is appropriate for situations where a 'final' system can be
developed only through an *adaptive* process of *learning* and evolution.

Steven Alter (1980)
DSS versus conventional EDP
Use: active vs. passive
User: line, staff and management vs. clerk
User goal: effectiveness vs. efficiency
Time horizon: present and future vs. past
System Objective: flexibility vs. consistency

Moore and Chang (1980)
DSS is an extensible system, capable of supporting adhoc data
analysis and decision modelling, oriented toward future *planning*, and used
at *irregular*, unplanned intervals.

Bonczek et al. (1980)
DSS consists of three *interacting components:* a language system, a
knowledge system and a problem processing system.

Bennett (1982)
A DSS is a *coherent* system of computer-based technology (hardware,
software and supporting documentation) used by managers as an aid in
semi-structured decision tasks.

Bui (1984)
DSS is a computer-based system that supports its *user(s)* to make
effective decisions in ill-structured problems.

Table 2.1. Evolution of Key Concepts in DSS Definition

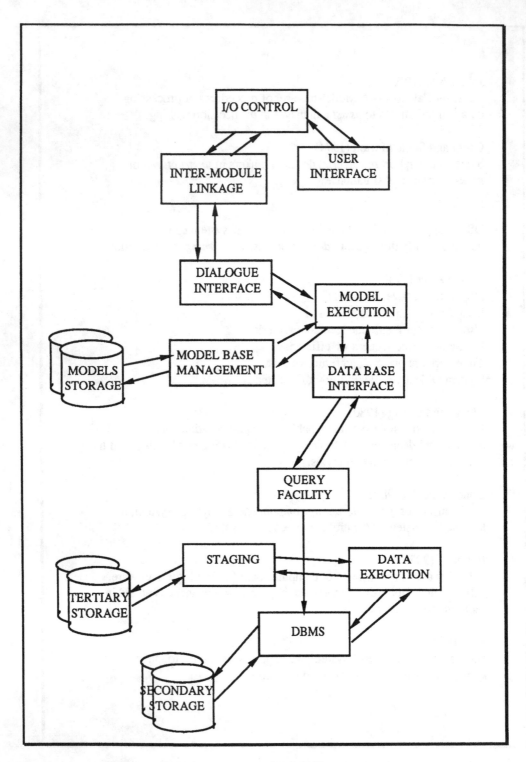

**Figure 2.2. A Schema of DSS Components
adapted from Ariav and Ginzberg (1986)**

Base Management is at least twofold: to ensure a logical independence between models and data and between models and user interfaces; and to enable manipulation of models (e.g., select, add/delete various models in the model base, restructuring existing models, generating new models). The Model Execution module 'arranges' logical sequences of computations; i.e., what model (or model subroutines) should be performed first. The two remaining units (Dialogue and Data Base interfaces) connect the Model Base component with the Dialogue component and the Data component.

One of the purposes of the *Data component* is to help the user select a set of data relevant to his decision problem. Again, the structure of the Data component is analogous to the two other components. It contains a Query Facility to permit dialogue with the user through the Dialogue component. This facility should make it easier for the decision maker to retrieve the data he needs to structure the problem. It will also include a Database Management System (DBMS) that allows the decision maker to add, delete, and generate data. Finally, a 'staging' system may be introduced to retrieve selective data from external sources of information (i.e., tertiary storage). This staging capability provides the DSS with data necessary to generate new alternatives, and to eventually bring new dimensions in the decision problem to the user. In effect, there usually exists a large number of feasible alternatives and the decision makers only know a few of them. At least from a theoretical viewpoint, the greater the decision space, (i.e., number of alternatives) the better the chance for the decision maker to find a satisfactory solution, given the costs of acquisition and storage as well as the risk of getting confused due to information overload.

2.2.2   Development Strategies

The DSS literature often refers to at least three types of DSS architecture: the *network*, the *bridge* and the *sandwich*. Figure 2.3 exhibits

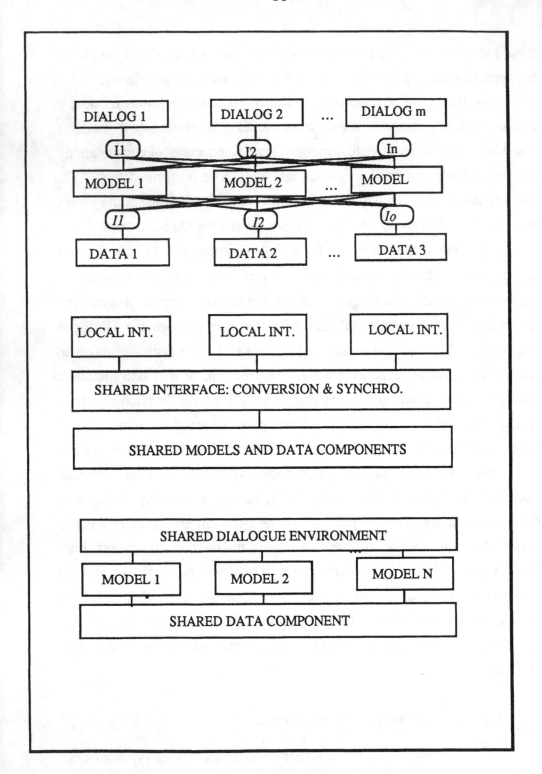

Figure 2.3. Three Possible DSS Architectures

	DSS Network	DSS Bridge	DSS Sandwich
ADVANTAGES	Ease of integration of independently developed components Localization of component interface codes (simplification of maintenance and extension) Flexibility for component sharing	Simplicity of technique thus reliable Ease of implementation of different types of modelling components	Ability to integrate a variety of previously separate decision support tools Ease for users to learn new tools
DISADVANTAGES	'Ease-of-Use' decreases when there is multiple dialogue components Performance decreases due to interface overhead and query Dependence on Operating System Reliability decreases because of multiplicity of interface	Possible performance problems	Difficulty to integrate external data (substantial data conversion effort) Restricted control interfaces All components must have the same operating environment

Table 2.2.   Advantages and Disadvantages of DSS Architectures

the fundamentals of these three architectures. Table 2.2 is a summary of some most important strengths and weaknesses of the component arrangements. To reduce the risk of falling short of the uncertain objectives of the system, DSS researchers often argue for the adoption of the adaptive design strategy and evolve the final system through *prototyping*. While adaptive design deals with continued (re)design of an evolving DSS, prototyping consists of an implementation methodology that focuses on the effort in building a quick and working prototype or model that has the minimum features, and meet the basic information requirements. This early system is then delivered to the end-user for evaluation. The users in turn give their feedback for determining possible enhancements (Naumann and Jenkins, 1982). The system builder studies the users' suggestions, redesign and update the prototype accordingly. This interaction between the users and the system builder continues until a satisfactory version is achieved. An important implication of such an iterative and evolutionary process is that both the user and the DSS builder are expected to make mistakes, but attempt to learn as much as possible from these mistakes. Thus, adaptive design involves the role of learning in the DSS building process. To further focus on the learning role, Bui and Sivasankaran (1987) suggest a technique that alerts the DSS builder's attention to infeasible aspects of the DSS early and helps him prioritize the DSS development sequence in such a way that the development risk is minimized. To estimate the likelihood of accomplishing the implementation of a DSS module, the technique seeks to elicit the user's perceived task structuredness and to judge the adequacy of tools available for DSS implementation.

2.3 GROUP DECISION-MAKING SITUATIONS

A collective decision-making process can be defined as a decision situation in which (i) there are two or more persons, each of them characterized by his or her own perceptions, attitudes, motivations, and personalities, (ii) who recognize the existence of a common problem, and (iii) attempt to reach a collective decision (Bui and Jarke, 1984). Furthermore, the group can interact simultaneously (i.e., pooled-interdependent mode) or make individual decisions separately and then collectively confront and discuss the results (i.e., sequential-interdependent mode).

One can observe three broad types of group decision-making: a single decision maker acting in a collective decision environment, cooperative decision-making, and non-cooperative decision-making.

In the *non-cooperative decision situation,* the decision makers play the role of antagonists or disputants. Conflict and competition are common forms of non-cooperative decision-making. While the former represents a situation in which disputants seek to hurt their opponents to pursue their own interests, the latter is characterized by the fact that each competitor is an action candidate, and is trying to outperform others (see also Section 11.1).

In the *group decision-making situation with one person,* a particular decision maker ultimately makes the decision and assumes responsibility for his line of action. However, the decision can be regarded as a collective one because of the existence of a dense network of influences that surrounds this single decision maker. In fact, other participants in the decision maker's organization can either support or act against the decision. Thus, the behavior and attitudes of other people who are indirectly involved in the decision-making process should be analyzed.

In a *cooperative environment,* the decision makers attempt to reach a common decision in a friendly and trusting manner, and share the responsibility. Consensus, negotiation, voting schemes, and even the recourse to a third party to dissolve differences are examples of this type of group decision-making.

Also, the literature in decision-making describes two types of decision situations involving more than one user: *pooled interdependent* and *sequential interdependent*. In a pooled decision-making situation, decision makers reunite together to form a more or less homogeneous group, and attempt to resolve a collective problem simultaneously. Elsewhere, in a sequential interdependent situation, members of the group can attack the collective problem at different periods in time, looking at different decision angles.

Another classification of group problem solving approach found in the literature (see Chapter 3) is the distinction between *content-oriented* and *process-oriented* approaches. The first approach focuses on the content of the problem, attempting to find an optimal or satisfactory solution given certain social or group constraints, or objectives. By contrast, the second approach is based on the observation that the group goes through certain phases in the group decision-making process, and on the belief that there could be an arranged way to effectively deal with these phases.

When a collective decision fails, it becomes necessary for the participants in the group problem solving to start bargaining or negotiating until a consensus is found. While *bargaining* involves discussion within a specific criterion or issues, *negotiation* includes many criteria or issues in the discussion and search for consensus.

2.4 COOPERATIVE MULTIPLE CRITERIA GROUP DECISION SUPPORT SYSTEMS

A cooperative multiple criteria group decision support system is a DSS (as defined in 2.3), that (i) contains MCDM and supporting models in the individual Model component, and (ii) is able to support multiple decision makers via a Group DSS to reach a consensus in a cooperative environment.

Section 2.1 described the characteristics and the general decision-making process of MCDM. Due to their peculiarity, MCDM seem to play a crucial role in supporting group decision-making:

1. Due to interpersonal differences, the existence of multiple and *conflicting objectives* is substantially more dominant in group decision-making than in single person decision-making;

2. *Subjective and qualitative assessments* seem to play a more crucial role in group than in single user decision-making. It has been observed that it is relatively easy for decision makers to agree upon problems that have objective, quantifiable and well-defined attributes. Conversely, decision makers tend to disagree upon attributes that require subjective and qualitative assessments. Furthermore, in group decision-making, in addition to the evaluation of the situational problem, decision makers invariably attempt to evaluate and the decision analyses of themselves and others.

3. The *simplicity of MCDM outputs* makes it easier to communicate, coordinate and aggregate individual analyses in the group decision-making process.

4. The *process* often plays a more decisive role than the *content* in group problem solving. MCDM provide a simple but structured framework for controlling the decision-making process, i.e., assessment of alternatives, assessment of evaluation criteria, selection of an appropriate algorithm for assessment of preferences, and search for a solution or compromise;

5.   The *division of decision processes* into four stages also allows alternate utilization of both objective optimization and subjective evaluation.

6.   The *iterative use* of the MCDM processes would permit integration of predecision and postdecision phases in the habitual decision phase.

Specifically, the Co-oP System reported in this research attempts to support the following decision situations:

1.   There are multiple users or decision makers. They may share an equal weight or have an unequal or 'hierarchically' distributed weight corresponding to a particular decision-making context. They can also divide their decision-making responsibilities according to their respective expertise. In other words, they can segment a group decision problem into (hierarchically) sequential single user decision problems according to individual expertise and responsibility.

2.   The group shares a common set of feasible decision alternatives that can be generated and collectively accepted from group members. From this set of alternatives, the decision makers can either select one or more alternatives, or rank them according to a given set of evaluation criteria.

3.   Each decision maker has his personal objectives that reflect a priori values and aspiration levels. Objectives are concretely expressed by criteria or attributes that are discrete, and at least ordinally measurable. Due to personal differences, individual decision outcomes – as opposed to a collective decision outcome that the

group is trying to reach an agreement on – often differ from one decision maker to the other.

4. The decision makers can be geographically dispersed and not required to log into the system at the same time. Via a distributed computer network system, they can communicate to others either sequentially or in an on-line mode.

5. The decision makers interact in a cooperative manner and in a trusting environment. The system does not handle attempts to cheat or to seek coalition within sub-groups. However, a third party can be invited to help the group resolve or dissolve conflicts. Electronic communication channels are available to support both structured and format-free information exchange between group members. The protocols governing the communications exchange (e.g., what type of information to be shared, who can or cannot receive information, etc.) can be set prior to the group problem solving process.

6. The decision makers can either work closely together by forming a homogeneous group that uses a single decision support system, or work independently and then proceed to a multilateral assessment of the problem.

7. When a consensus is not found, negotiable alternatives are sought – if any – to offer group members new perspectives for further analyses.

SUMMARY

The purpose of this chapter was to define basic concepts that underlie multiple criteria decision methods, decision support systems, and the context of cooperative multiple criteria group DSS in group decision-making situations.

Despite the multitude of algorithms found in multiple criteria decision methods, MCDM processes can be invariably broken into four steps: (i) identification and definition of alternatives, (ii) identification and definition of evaluation criteria, (iii) evaluation of alternatives according to criteria, and (iv) use of an algorithm to search for a solution.

Attempt to design multiple criteria DSS implies integration of MCDM methods into more elaborated dialogue interface and data base management. Furthermore, expanding MCDM to support group decision-making accentuates the differentiation between content-oriented and process-oriented approaches to decision-making. Such an extension also requires consideration of additional frameworks that help understand and resolve group decision-making such as aggregation of preferences and consensus seeking.

Before elaborating on the requirements analysis and design issues for cooperative multiple criteria group DSS, it is necessary to review important work related to collective decision-making.

3. REVIEW OF PRIOR RELATED RESEARCH: A DSS ENGINEERING PERSPECTIVE

The problem of collective decision-making has been extensively investigated by numerous researchers. Most of this work could be classified into two main streams of research. The first approach focuses on the content of the problem, attempting to find an optimal or satisfactory solution given certain social or group constraints, or objectives. By contrast, the second approach is process-oriented. It is based on the observation that the group goes through certain phases in the group decision-making process, and on the belief that there could be an arranged way to effectively deal with these phases. Behavioral studies are part of the research devoted to this process-oriented approach. More recently, a third approach to group problem solving has emerged from the Decision Support System technology. This chapter successively discusses these three approaches, and examines to what extent they can be used as a requirements analysis framework for designing multiple criteria group decision support system.

3.1 CONTENT-ORIENTED APPROACHES

Despite the large number of literature on MCDM (see for example, Zeleny (1982)), for a recent collection of bibliographies), attempts to develop multiple criteria decision methods for multiple users are recent and rather scarce. Thiriez and Houri (1975), Bereanu (1975), Keeney and Kirkwood (1975), Barclay and Peterson (1976), Kenney (1976), Edwards (1977), Wendell (1979), Korhonen et al. (1980) and Moskowitz et al.

(1981), Zeleny (1982), and Heidel and Duckstein (1983), Seo (1984) are among the few that have introduced the problem of multiple users in multiple criteria decision-making. These multiple user MCDM are deeply influenced by the research on aggregation of preferences or by game theory (for example, see von Winterfeldt and Edwards, 1986). Therefore, the foundations of MU-MCDM can hardly be understood without discussing the theory of elections and social choice and the game theoretic approach.

3.1.1   The Theory of Elections and Social Choice

The first content-oriented approach to collective decision-making originates from the theory of elections of the eighteenth century, and have evolved into the social choice theory of today.

The oldest theory of elections is probably due to Condorcet (1775). Given a number of available candidates from whom only one is elected, Condorcet proposes a pairwise comparison scheme, and suggests that the candidate who receives a majority of votes against every other candidate should be elected. Borda (1781) suggests that each elector (i.e., decision maker) establishes an ordinal ranking, and defines the collective decision as the sum of the ranks assigned by each of the electors (see also section 5.2.). Kendall (1962) extends the ordinal ranking problem in a statistical framework. He defines a ranking correlation coefficient that estimates the true ranking, given some agreements among the observers or experts, and the accuracy of their judgments. Due to its computational simplicity the Borda-Kendall technique is widely used to determine consensus ranking.

Another classical contribution to the area of collective decision-making is the work by Edgeworth (1881). By defining welfare as how well off the individuals in society feel (this definition is also called 'individualistic assumption' which is by no means universally accepted (Nicholson, 1978)), the necessary condition for a social optimum is to obtain a Pareto (1896) optimal allocation of resources (one in which no one can be made better off without making someone else worse off). Thus, in the familiar Edgeworth box diagram for exchange, only the points on the contract curve represent efficient social allocations, and are eligible to be considered as possible candidates for a social optimum. Assuming that individual utilities are measurable, a utility possibility frontier that represents all possible efficient combinations of utility that the society can achieve, can be derived from the contract curve. Further, if one postulates the existence of a social welfare function, it is possible to conceptualize the sufficient condition of the problem of social choice, i.e., to maximize social welfare. However, the maximization of social welfare leads to a difficult policy choice between efficiency and equity.

A general theory of collective choice was missing until Arrow's (1963) social welfare axioms were elaborated. The axioms are: (i) Complete ordering, (ii) responsiveness to individual preferences, (iii) non-imposition, (iv) non-dictatorship and (v) independence of irrelevant alternatives. Arrow proves that, in general, there is no procedure for obtaining a group ordering that satisfies the five axioms. In other words, a collective decision cannot be made without violating one or more of the above mentioned axioms (known as Arrow's Impossibility Theorem).

Arrow's work has generated continued attention on group preference axiomatization for dealing with the consensus ranking problem. Quirk and Saposnik (1962), Kemeny and Snell (1962), Inada (1969), Bowman and Colantoni (1973), Bogart (1973, 1975), Young (1974, 1977), Cook and Seiford (1978, 1982), and Armstrong et al. (1982) are among a host of authors that pursue this ordinal ranking and consensus formation framework. Fishburn (1971), Mueller (1976) and Plott (1976) provide elaborate reviews of the social welfare literature.

In sum, the large number of studies on collective decision-making provide a useful framework for demonstrating particular aspects of the problem of social choice. However, many political theorists argue that it is neither impossible nor desirable to search for a unique and universally acceptable formulation of collective choice. As an implication for this research, a methodological framework to help select appropriate group decision techniques remains desirable.

3.1.2   The Game-Theoretic Approach

Another approach for content-oriented collective decision-making is the game-theoretic approach. A 'classical' game can be defined by the following characteristics: (i) pure conflict or antagonistic games (each player operates on the basis of self-interest); (ii) complete information (the players know their own and others utility functions and strategies); (iii) mutual expected rationality (each player follows certain rationality postulates, expects and acts on the expectation that other player will do the same); (iv) non-cooperative; and (v) absence of delayed commitment (no strategies may be changed after one or more individual moves have been made).

In a two-person classical setting, von Neumann and Morgenstern (1953) argue that the rationality on the part of both players will lead them to adopt minimax strategies (i.e., minimum of possible maximal gains). These strategies are equilibrium strategies (also called saddle point) in that each player would have done worse by choosing differently. The Neumann-Morgenstern equilibrium strategies were however quickly challenged by Tucker (Luce and Raiffa, 1957). In addition to the fact that not all 'matrix' games have saddle points, Tucker shows that individual rationality in an uncertain situation can lead to a result that is collectively irrational. Tucker's 'prisoner's dilemma' is a prototype of many real life decision situations.

When the game is expanded to more than two persons (n-person games), it becomes considerably more complex because of the possibility of forming coalitions among the players. The concept of coalition leads to the cooperative game.

The cooperative game is the game in which the players join binding agreements. These agreements may be aimed at coordinating strategies or sharing payoffs. In both types of agreement, the analysis is often very complex. First, unless there is perfect agreement between players (which is a trivial case), partial agreement is difficult to formulate. Second, sharing payoffs is not always possible, given the non-transferability of certain payoffs (Jones, 1980). Thus, the problem is distribution of the payoffs (i.e., gains or losses) among the parties in a manner which is acceptable or enforceable. The von Neumann-Morgenstern theory of solutions for n-person games in characteristic function form was the first comprehensive mathematical model for studying such coalition games. This theory has in turn generated a large number of models and techniques. Tucker et al. (eds.) (1950, 1953, 1957, 1959 and 1964) and Case (1979) give excellent bibliographies. It is worth noting that the existence of a stable core of solutions in a classical cooperative game induced by the von Neumann-Morgenstern theorem is related to that of Edgeworth's contract curve in welfare economics.

The classical game theory proves to be hardly practical (Wierzbicki, 1983), and even less useful for our scope of study. First, computational techniques for finding solutions to specific games are burdensome for the parties who are interested in putting game theory into practice. Second, empirical conflict situations are rarely characterized by decision makers with a single objective. Last but not least, it is too 'demanding' to require mutual expected rationality from the decision makers.

3.2 PROCESS-ORIENTED APPROACHES

The interactive procedures found in Operations Research/Management Science (OR/MS) and the organizational psychology approach can both be viewed as process-oriented approaches in that they focus on the decision-making dynamics. However, the methodology differs. While the first methodology can be more or less viewed as a dynamic version of the content-oriented approach mostly based on utility theory (e.g., Farquhar, 1984; Fishburn, 1984), the second focuses on the evolution of the decision makers' behavior and the use of appropriate negotiation skills during the group decision-making processes.

3.2.1   Interactive Procedures

Some single-user MCDM look at the process-oriented approach as a learning process. Based on the assumption that the decision maker's preferences form and evolve with a particular decision situation, these MCDM strive to help the user progressively articulate his preferences. Geoffrion, Dyer, and Feinberg (1972), Dyer (1972), Dyer and Wehrung (1973), Hall and Haimes (1976), Zionts and Wallenius (1976), Hwang and Masud (1979) are examples of methods that rely on the idea of interactive conversational computer-based systems to enhance communication, interpretation and modification of results. Steuer (1979), Steuer and Schuler (1978), and Morse (1980) use methods that progressively eliminate non-dominated alternatives, and thus help the decision maker focus on a more manageable set of alternatives. Jacquet-Lagreze and Shakun (1984) propose an interactive additive utility technique that aids the decision maker in the sharpening of his situation-dependent, circumstance-shaped, evolving preference patterns. Evans (1984) provides an overview of these techniques and their variations.

However, the learning process embedded in the MCDM mentioned above can be viewed as a dynamic aspect – and particularly a learning process – of the content-oriented approach, and more importantly deals mostly with a single decision maker. Rao and Shakun (1974), Shakun (1981a, 1981b), Chartterjee and Ulvila (1982) are among those who propose a dynamic model to tackle bargaining and negotiations. For example, by defining conflict as a dynamic problem that initially does not have a feasible solution, Shakun refers to conflict resolution as redefinition of the problem so that there is a collective solution for the redefined problem. Search for new alternatives or alteration of aspiration levels are examples of problem redefinition (Tietz, 1983). These concepts do provide a necessary framework for designing evolutionary systems (e.g., group decision support system), but require more operational tools for practical applications.

3.2.2   Organizational Psychology

Another group decision process-oriented framework can be found in behavioral scientists' work. Bales (1955), Bales and Strodtbeck (1951), Chamberlain and Kuhn (1965), Walton and McKensie (1965), Warr (1973), Litterer (1966), Krauss and Deutsch (1966), Deutsch (1973), Vroom and Jago (1974), Zartman (ed, 1978), Wall (1981), Bacharach and Lawler, 1981) are among numerous researchers who study various behavioral modes dealing with group problem solving, bargaining and negotiation. Persuasion, bridging, assertion, and attraction are usual relevant influence skills that the decision makers are recommended to manipulate in negotiation. Walton (1969), Rubin and Brown (1975), Pruitt (1981), Rubin (1981) and other social psychologists emphasize the importance of creating a favorable group discussion environment (e.g., processes of communication, site for discussion, composition of the meeting, deadlines, etc.). Fogg presents a repertoire of creative and peaceful approaches to deal with conflicts (Fogg, 1985). Creative approaches not only seek compromise basic demands but try to satisfy the involved parties beyond their needs. Levy (1985) examines the dynamics of moving a deadlock toward a cooperative resolution. He argues that there exists a cooperation threshold that reflects the degree of certainty of achieving a cooperative outcome. Such a threshold must be reached to induce cooperation.

However, the success of the techniques that can affect or influence the group decision processes have so far relied entirely on the abilities of trained negotiators or on a skillful third party who intervenes in a conflict settlement. From a GDSS standpoint at least, it would be useful to automate some of these techniques in the DSS for cooperative group decision-making.

3.3 INFORMATION SYSTEMS APPROACHES

Recently, information systems technology has increasingly attracted MCDM researchers who strive to implement their MCDM. Recent symposia on MCDM show a growing interest in Decision Support System technology to build a more effective MCDM (Bui, 1984; Keeny et al., 1986). At least from a theoretical viewpoint, the DSS-MCDM connection seems to be promising. DSS technology can turn MCDM – that are still too mathematical and too formal – into a supportive tool that can effectively fit the decision makers' needs. This section reviews some design issues in DSS that could be useful for our framework, and expands the discussion to some of the findings in telecommunications. Unlike MCDM and DSS that have focused more on a single decision maker, telecommunications research has attempted to measure the effects of electronic media on handling interpersonal interaction and communication.

3.3.1 Decision Support Systems

In section 2.2, basic concepts of decision support systems were briefly reviewed. Also, in a previous paper, we have discussed the effective use of the DSS approach to build MCDM and have indicated a substantial number of DSS-related publications (Bui, 1984). An effective DSS often possesses the following characteristics: (i) emphasis on semistructured and ill-structured decisions, (ii) support and improvement of decision-making, (iii) ability to serve multiple users, (iv) support of all phases of the decision-making process, and (v) ease-of-use (Sprague and Carlson, 1982; Bennett, 1983). Despite the substantial amount of literature on DSS, few of them explicitly deal with group decision support (Stohr, 1981), and even less with organizational decision support.

Bonzeck et al. (1979) propose some guidelines for building computer-based systems to support organization decision-making. Based on the assumption that the organization is a multi-level network of specialized decision makers, they hypothesize that a computerized decision support for organization should be able to identify all information processors required in a decision-making process and a division of labor between them. A artificial intelligence framework and/or a database model could then be built to reduce data, formulate models and generate some facts or expectations about a specific group problem under consideration. More specifically, Hackathorn and Keen (1981) describe two types of decision situations involving more than one user: pooled interdependent and sequential interdependent. While the former is nothing but the minimal form of collective decision-making that works well only with homogeneous and knowledgeable groups, the latter gives autonomy and flexibility to each individual member of the group. Carlson and Sutton (1974), Holloway and Mantey (1976), Saaty (1980), Steeb and Johnston (1981), Gray (1981, 1983), Bui and Jarke (1984), Hart et al. (1985), Applegate et al. (1987) and Stefik et al. (1987) present examples of decision support systems that involve multiple decision makers. A common profile of all of these systems is the attempt to decompose the group decision-making process into a series of tasks to be supported. These tasks include brainstorming, structuring, planning, discussion, evaluation, voting, consensus seeking, etc. Although most GDSS reported follow the general sequence of group decision-making process, the emphasis of computerized support differs from one to another due principally to the technology adopted (e.g., GDSS setting, group decision technique used, etc.). It remains to be empirically proven that such GDSS can truly support all group problem solving tasks, since they mostly deal with the pooled type of group decision-making which is only a minimal form of collective decision-making.

In an attempt to focus on the interaction issues of computer based group problem solving, Huber (1984) – and, in the same line of reasoning, DeSanctis and Gallupe (1985, 1987) – emphasize the role of GDSS as group facilitator. These authors argue that a GDSS should be generalized enough to increase the frequency of use, and consequently, the likelihood of GDSS use for group decision-making. Huber also advocates that process-oriented communications such as textual and relational information are more important for GDSS than for individual DSS. Vogel et al. (1987) expand the focus on issues related to system facility (i.e., setting, hardware, software), group characteristics (i.e., size, composition, experience, task) and facilitation (i.e., technical competence, group skills). However, further studies are needed to prove how these arguments could be translated into the design of an effective GDSS.

Another approach that attempts tackling GDSS applies artificial intelligence methods to the analysis and design of generalized, application independent Model Management Systems. This approach has emerged in the last five years (e.g., Elam et al., 1980; Bonczek et al., 1980, Konsynski and Dolk, 1982; Dolk, 1983; Whinston, 1984, Applegate et al. 1987). The underlying philosophy of Model Management Systems (MMS) is to allow the model component of a DSS to handle models in the same way that a database management system (DBMS) handles data, i.e., application-independent, knowledge-based, and able to support multiple views of models. As an attempt to import expert systems approach to DSS, Licker and Thompson (1985) implemented a 'GDSS by one person' called PROMAD. In fact, PROMAD is no more than an individual DSS that can store opinions and expertise pooled from groups of persons involved in a decision problem. Jarke et al. (1985) suggest a more complete data-centered approach whose principal functions are to provide the decision makers with relational and integrated view of individual results.

3.3.2   Telecommunications and Office Information Systems

The analysis, design and implementation of multiple user DSS could not be done without considering the developing technology in computer networks and studies on the effects of electronic communication media on human interaction. Traditional communication channels (e.g., correspondence, telephone, and face-to-face) are now supplemented with electronic mail, teleconferencing and video conferencing. Although executives continue to prefer oral and face-to-face communications for their work, distributed environments have slowly taken place.

From a *technological* standpoint, Martin (1981) and Tanenbaum (1981), among others, provide a comprehensive discussion of computer networks and distributed processing. The unique characteristic of a distributed system is that each of the geographically separated computers in the network can process independent application programs, while sharing communication facilities. A growing literature on various aspects of the design, implementation, use and management of computer networks can also be found in a recent journal – Computer Networks. While computer scientists predict that computer networks will be cheaper and easier to use, they also recognize that the related technology is rapidly changing. In order to cope with this rapidly changing trend, one would argue for the design of a group decision support system that is independent of the computer network technology.

From a *managerial* standpoint, scientists in the organization behavior area suggested that the major issue is to identify factors that dictate the successful implementation and acceptance of new communication channels (Johansen et Bullen, 1984; Trauth et al. 1984). Short et al. (1976); Johansen et al. (1979), and Christie (1981) provide discussions on recent field studies of the impacts of electronic media (e.g., audio, video, computer conferencing as alternatives to face-to-face meetings). More specifically, they found that it is possible for each member of a group to participate more actively in a computer conference than in a face-to-face meeting. In the latter form of meeting, only one person can speak at a time, and the most dominant person often monopolizes the discussion.

Williams (1978) observes that teleconferences have been less emotional in tone than face-to-face communications. It was also found that teleconferences are better suited for explicit information exchange than bargaining and negotiation (Dutton et al., 1982) and video conferencing has greater information capacity than the telephone but is less rich than face-to-face.

Also, laboratory findings by Wichman (1970), Dorris et al. (1972), Short (1974) on the effects of various media on conflict, bargaining games (e.g., prisoner's dilemma game), attitude change during conflict resolution processes have indicated that conflict is an area particularly sensitive to the medium of communication. Among other things, they found (i) a positive relationship between the number of communication channels and the degree of cooperation, and (ii) a positive relationship between the efficiency of the interaction (i.e., speed and/or accuracy of communication) and the degree of cooperation.

However, due to the complex nature of conflict, laboratory procedures, there have been repeated inconclusive, and even conflicting results on these empirical studies. Nevertheless, some of the most convergent findings can be used as guidelines to design communication channels and user interfaces for group DSS discussed in later chapters.

SUMMARY

The literature surveyed in this chapter demonstrated the strong interest among researchers from various disciplines to tackle group decision-making and group decision support systems. It also underlined the complexity of the problem that has led to a lack of, or impossibility to define, a general and coherent approach to group decision problem.

From a group DSS perspective, the sophistication of the game theoretic approach – as well as its restrictive assumptions – has discouraged the average decision maker. Also, discussions on the theory of elections and social choice seem to suggest a pragmatic avenue to group problem solving. Ordinal and cardinal rankings remain basic elements for determining collective choice. However, defining collective norms that are specific to a particular context has become a requisite for a satisfactory use of group decision techniques.

Moreover, growing findings by organizational psychologists as well as early attempts to design computer based MCDM and group DSS seem to emphasize on the process of group decision-making. The analysis of this process ranges from the understanding of various media (e.g., electronic communication media, or human mediator) to the use of information systems technology (e.g., DSS and artificial intelligence). It remains, however, unclear how these findings can be systematically pooled together to formulate a synthetic approach to group decision support. As a point of departure, a better understanding of the roles and functions of decision support systems in group decision-making would help DSS researchers concentrate their effort on the most crucial group decision support issues and on the continued identification of computer technology for GDSS use.

4. THE FUNCTIONS AND ROLES OF DSS IN GROUP DECISION-MAKING

The roles of a DSS represent the potential impact it causes on decision-making; its functions specify the services it offers to its user. In group problem solving, the roles and functions of a DSS cannot, however, be defined as if in a single user environment because of the complex nature of human interaction. As a framework for discussion, this chapter suggests six possible types of DSS-user interactions. It then attempts to identify new roles and functions of DSS in a multiple user decision-making environment. It particularly emphasizes the existence of a dichotomy of roles, and of a multiple functionality of DSS in group decision-making.

4.1 A TYPOLOGY OF GROUP DSS

Regardless of the type of group decision-making discussed earlier, one can envision six possible types of DSS-user interactions (Figure 4.1).

Type 1 represents the traditional DSS paradigm. The purpose of such a DSS is to enhance the user's cognitive processing capabilities and/or to facilitate the learning process. The bilateral relationship between user and DSS provides no communications support as required in cooperative decision-making. In fact, this type of DSS has been criticized for its potential isolating role (Sanders et al., 1984).

In type 2, a group of users has access to a traditional DSS, typically through an intermediary. The purpose of such a DSS is in essence the same as the single user DSS. Tasks that are specific to group decision-making

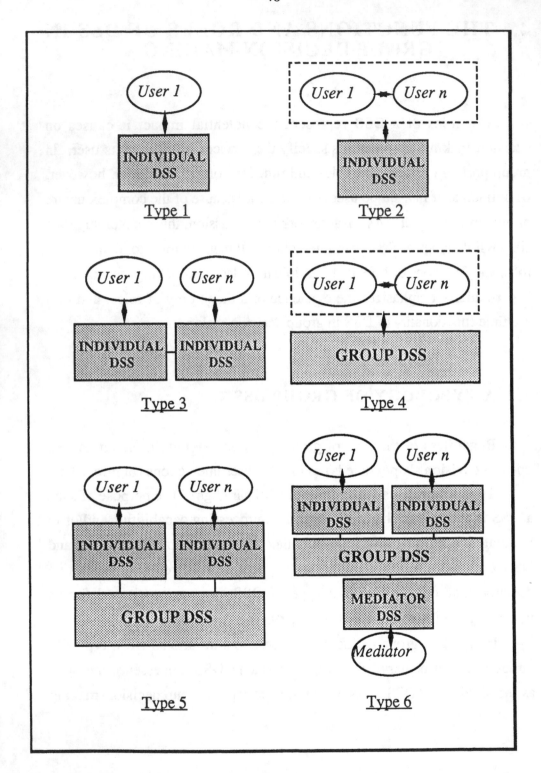

Figure 4.1. A Typology of Group DSS

process (e.g., discussion, aggregation of preferences or votes) remain unsupported by the DSS.

The third possible GDSS architecture (Type 3) includes the capabilities of the previous ones but also provides computerized or automated some group problem solving capabilities (e.g., automated computation of aggregation of preferences, electronic interpretation of individual votes). The relationship between the decision group and the GDSS still remains but is bilateral since they share the same man-machine interface. This type of GDSS is exemplified by Huber's (1982) decision room approach, and the single-user, multiplayer DSS by Licker and Thompson (1985).

While the third architecture provides a mechanism for mapping and integrating application-level communications results (i.e., preference aggregation and mediation support), another generalization of the individual DSS framework (Type 4) addresses the need for knowledge sharing among remote individual DSS, for instance, by exchanging data files or mail messages. However, this network of loosely coupled individual DSS lacks knowledge about the existence of a decision group. The role of the GDSS is reduced to installing and supporting communications activities. Computer teleconferencing, and to some extent, video and audio teleconferencing, and remote electronic bulletin boards, can be classified into this GDSS architecture.

Type 5 and 6 suggest a multilateral relationship between members of a group via a network of individual DSS and group DSS. The functions of such a network of DSS are to support both the decision maker who is a member of the group and the group itself. However, only individual users interact with the system; the group as a whole is no longer a single user of the GDSS. In other words, the fifth and sixth types of GDSS represent a distributed problem solving composed by a decentralized, loosely coupled group of decision makers.

This classification is valid for any group size. From a system design point of view, increasing the number of group members will only result in coupling additional communication channels between DSS nodes. From the GDSS use point of view, experience suggests that GDSS efficiency increases as the size of the group increases (Bui et al., 1987; Vogel et al., 1987).

The last two types of GDSS can be further expanded according to various structures for decision-making. Figure 4.2 illustrates five variances of multiple user decision structures. It also suggests expected impacts of these structures on the speed and correctness of the decision-making process (HEAT, 1983). It has been found that, in general, the star configuration seems to be the most effective to handle both structured and ill-structured problems (HEAT, 1983), whereas, the wheel configuration seems to be slightly more appropriate for creative or unstructured decision situations.

4.2 THE DICHOTOMY OF ROLES AND FUNCTIONS IN GDSS

The multiple relationship of DSS shown in Figure 4.1-5 and 4.1-6 is characterized by a dichotomy of roles (Figure 4.3). On the one hand, each of the individual DSS strives to be (i) individual-oriented (i.e., it should be as personal as possible to its single user), (ii) partial (i.e., it should favor its user in negotiating with other members of the group), and (iii) permanent or semi-permanent (i.e., it should accompany and evolve with its user over the decision-making time span).

Three functions can be envisaged in a individual DSS: (i) generalized and unified decision support for individual decision-making, (ii) communication support, and (iii) negotiation support for assisting the individual in negotiating with other decision makers of the group.

| GDSS Configuration | Group Decision Making Characteristics | | | |
| | Formatted | | Free-Format | |
	Speed	Correctness	Speed	Correctness
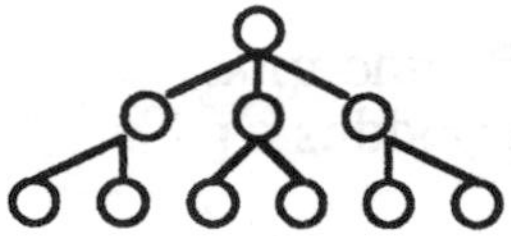 HIERARCHICAL	HIGH	MEDIUM	HIGH	LOW
 STAR	HIGH	HIGH	HIGH	MEDIUM TO HIGH
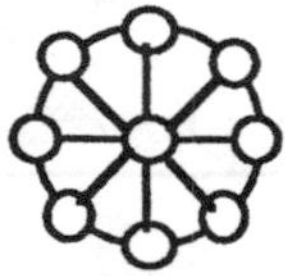 WHEEL	LOW TO MEDIUM	HIGH	MEDIUM TO HIGH	HIGH
 HONEYCOMB	MEDIUM	LOW	LOW	LOW
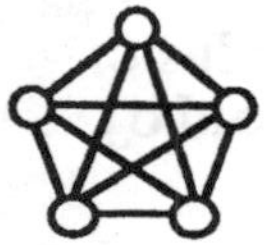 MULTI-CONNECTED	LOW	HIGH	MEDIUM	HIGH

Figure 4.2. Five Variances of GDSS Decision Structures and their Impacts on Decision Outcomes (adapted from HEAT, 1983)

	INDIVIDUAL DSS	GROUP DSS
ROLES	To provide a personalized tool to support individual decision-maker(s) To promote 'partiality' Semi-permanent or permanent	To provide a 'universal' tool to support collective decision making To promote 'impartiality' Ad-hoc or semi-permanent
FUNCTIONS	To guide use of appropriate decision tools To support 'electronic' communications (e.g., electronic mail) To support its user to negotiate with other group members To simulate group decision making scenarios	To guide select group decision techniques (e.g., aggregation of preferences) To provide communication services (e.g., bulletin board) To solve, resolve or dissolve individual differences.

Figure 4.3. Dichotomy of Roles and Functions in Group Decision Support Systems

On the other hand, the primary roles of the group DSS are (i) to monitor and coordinate the relationships among participants either by promoting communication to reconcile differences or by limiting unnecessary or emotional interaction, (ii) to promote impartiality regarding the positions of the disputants and the outcomes, (iii) to be either permanent (i.e., once implemented the group DSS becomes a stable and formal collective procedure), or temporary (i.e., the DSS is an ad-hoc intervention).

The group DSS can provide four main functions: (i) monitoring of data exchange, (ii) automatic selection of appropriate group decision technique(s) unless the group overrides this procedure, (iii) computation and explanation of a group decision, and (iv) suggestion for a discussion of individual differences or for a redefinition of the problem if attempts to reach consensus fail.

The difference between the type 5 and type 6 GDSS is the existence of a human mediator in the computer-based group decision-making process in type 6. In type 5, the group problem solving processes stored in the Group DSS unit are activated according to some pre-defined norms.

The main function of the mediator oriented DSS is to personally help the mediator assess the group decision situation, and hence monitor the group DSS; the human mediator can either (i) seek to impartially resolve a dispute or (ii) be a judge who wants to end a conflict by imposing legal rules. Two additional functions could be envisaged for a mediator's GDSS.. First, the GDSS should help the mediator influence the structure (i.e., the way individual DSS are connected) and process (i.e., how individuals communicate between them) of communications. Second, it should assist the mediator collect and synchronize results (Jarke et al., 1985), identify individual differences as well as shared interests (Bartunek et al., 1977), and generate new issues and alternatives.

4.3 DYNAMICS OF GROUP DECISION SUPPORT

4.3.1   Group Problem Solving Activities and GDSS

Bales and Strodtbeck (1951) were among the first who observed five main types of functional problems during a group decision-making process. These typical activities include various tasks that a member of a group performs. They were classified by Benne and Sheats (1948) and they have been confirmed by a large number of recent empirical studies that replicate Bales and his colleagues' findings (e.g., Pye et al., 1973).

(1)   **Problem of orientation**: The decision makers often ignore, or are uncertain about, some of the relevant facts. They seek information, orientation, or confirmation. They establish rapport, share ideal values, identify common interests and objectives. Supporting the orientation problem would consist of facilitating information exchange between decision makers. In turn, this would assist decision makers formulate a collective problem, and elaborate group norms or rules of conduct during the decision-making process.

(2)   **Problem of evaluation**: The decision makers – because of their personalities, and the nature of the problem – have different values and interests. They need a personalized framework to individually analyze the problem and express their wishes and feelings.

(3)   **Problem of control**: Decision makers within the group may express different decision outcomes. They seek exchange of points of view, diagnose boundaries of the conflict, define a set of possible compromises in which each party makes some concessions, agree to work toward a solution, and find directions to reach a consensus among the feasible alternatives.

(4) **Problem of tension management:** The frequencies of both negative and positive reactions tend to increase during the group decision-making process. The group seeks to improve understanding, increase compliance, reduce tension, and avoid member withdrawal.

(5) **Problem of integration:** The group seeks solidarity during the group problem solving process, offers mutual concessions and collective endorsement of the final agreement.

While the problem of evaluation (Type 2) often remains the most frequent activity during a decision-making process, the problem of orientation (Type 1) is often prevalent at the beginning, whereas the problems of control (Type 3), tension management (Type 4), and integration (Type 5) are more frequent towards the end of the process.

4.3.2   GDSS as a Mediation Support

In a strict sense, consensus requires unanimity. In a more lenient sense, consensus needs only to reflect the desire of the majority which results from democratic processes. Usually, consensus cannot be reached in the first round of the group decision and negotiations become necessary to resolve individual differences.

Negotiations aim to either resolve or dissolve conflict. When individual differences exist, conflict resolution consists of finding concessions among members in order to reach a consensus. Thus, a group DSS should be able to suggest the decision makers what to negotiate (i.e., the contents of the problem) and how to convey these contents (i.e., the processes of the problem).

Conversely, when attempts to obtain concessions from the decision maker(s) fail, conflicts should be dissolved. The idea underlying conflict dissolution is characterized by the process of adaptive change. The decision makers not only attempt to redefine their objectives (Yu, 1981), but also search for new alternatives (Jantsch, 1967; Shakun, 1981a, 1981b). Group DSS should support iterative decision-making to facilitate problem redefinition.

The process of problem redefinition could be activated by first identifying existing issues and alternatives, and then by generating new issues and alternatives.

(1) Identification of existing issues and alternatives

The easiest approach to identifying existing issues is to collect information about the decision makers' expectations and constraints with regard to the problem. A GDSS should help decision makers collect, select, join, and supply missing data to focus on important and real issues (Simkin, 1971). A data-centered GDSS – such as the MEDIATOR concept (Jarke et al., 1985) – should be able to provide such functions.

Another function would consist of ranking issues (e.g., evaluation criteria) in descending order of importance to locate the size and scope of individual differences (Stevens, 1963). This would, in turn, allow the GDSS to highlight group members' common interests, and more importantly, to warn, at the early stages of the negotiations, about the danger of some issues that may lead to irrevocable disagreement.

(2) Generation of new issues and alternatives

Generating new issues and alternatives is often considered a last recourse in order to break a conflicting impasse. There are a number of ways that a mediator can generate new issues and alternatives solutions. Fisher (1984) suggests a technique called 'conflict fractionation'. This consists of breaking an unresolved monolithic issue into smaller manageable (sub-)issues that had not previously come to the protagonists' mind. Laboratory studies (e.g., Fisher, 1978; Froman and Cohen, 1970) as well as real life observations (Zeleny, 1982) clearly demonstrate that group decision problems that imply multiple issues have a greater chance to be resolved than the ones that revolve around a unique issue.

Sherif and Sherif (1969) propose the introduction of 'superordinate' issues or goals that are of shared concern to all parties. By introducing transcendent objectives, disputants who were competitive, probably become more cooperative. This, in turn, will facilitate a dispute settlement. Last but not least, Pruitt (1981) observes that one cause of dispute impasse is the 'overcommitment' of a group member to one or many issues. The mediator can request new priority that overrules or invalidates prior commitment.

Theoretically speaking, the results obtained from conflict dissolution are expected to be better than the ones provided by conflict resolution, since new alternatives, new objectives are likely to yield a better choice. However, scarcity of resources and time limit are some of the constraints that prevent an indefinite move towards conflict dissolution.

SUMMARY

Six types of group DSS architectures were discussed in this chapter. They differ in the way decision makers interact with each other via the DSS. This typology in turn helped differentiate the roles and functions of individual DSS and group DSS. The fundamental difference seems to originate from the fact that individual DSS provide personalized tools to support individual decision-making, whereas group DSS seek 'universal' norms to help search for common ground or better yet, collective consensus.

In addition, the types of group decision activities, as well as the nature of mediation support, advocated particular attention to the design of group DSS that help group members follow through various decision processes. The latter could be viewed as the vertebral column that intertwines a variety of content-oriented decision models along the entire collective decision-making process.

5. DESIGN ISSUES FOR THE GDSS MODEL COMPONENT

The decomposition of the group decision-making process into five types of problems — orientation, evaluation, control, tension management and integration — suggests a division of tasks within the group DSS functions, as well as a decomposition of the DSS model component. In this chapter, Section 5.1 advocates two strategies for designing the GDSS model component. First, it argues that the GDSS model component should support both process-oriented and content-oriented decision tasks. Second, it supports decomposition of the group DSS into two model bases: a model base for individual decision models and a model base for group decision techniques.

For the group decision model base, sections 5.2, 5.3 and 5.4 respectively review major content-oriented and process-oriented group decision techniques. In the context of individual multiple criteria decision-making, this chapter addresses design issues for building a unified MCDM decision support system. These elements include (i) the necessity to support a wide range of MCDM problems (section 5.5.1), (ii) the frequent need to partition group decision tasks (section 5.5.3), (iii) the difficulties and costs related to information searches (section 5.5.2), and the increasing difficulty in using integrated decision models (section 5.6).

5.1 MODULARIZATION OF GROUP DSS TASKS

5.1.1   Content-oriented and Process-oriented Methods

There are at least two arguments in favor of a division of the modeling tasks between content-oriented and process-oriented tasks, and a possibility to intertwine these tasks in the group decision-making process.

First, despite the efforts of the content-oriented DSS technology to help decision makers structure their initially unstructured problem, some unstructured parts will remain. This partial 'unstructurability' is due to uncertainty, fuzziness, ignorance, and an inability to quantitatively measure the complexity of the decision situation and the decision makers' preferences (Stohr, 1981).

Second, attempts to resolve a group decision problem are rendered more difficult by human irrationality and emotionality when dealing with group interaction (Pruitt, 1981). It is then necessary to search for some process-oriented methods that can support the ill-structured part left by the content-oriented DSS, as well as for some communication system that collects, coordinates, and disseminates information within the group.

There is no doubt that defining the boundaries of structurable and unstructurable problems is theoretically difficult. It is also difficult to determine whether a process-oriented approach or a content-oriented approach is best suited for solving a particular decision problem. However, since the problem of evaluation (i.e., type 2 described in 4.3.1) is likely to be structurable, it could be practically handled by content-oriented methods. Meanwhile, the problems of orientation, control, tension management, and integration (e.g., types (1), (3), (4), and (5)) – that are not structurable or less structurable – could probably be best taken care of by process-oriented methods (Bui and Jarke, 1984).

5.1.2   Individual Model Base and Group   Model Base

The dichotomy of DSS roles in group decision-making discussed in section 4.1 implicitly assumes the decomposition of a group DSS into individual and group decision support (sub-)systems. Furthermore, Cyert and March (1963) observe that group decision-making within organizations is often sequentially performed by different decision makers assuming different levels of expertise (e.g., nature of information possessed) and responsibility, using different decision-making approaches (e.g., optimization or heuristics).

Therefore, a DSS for collective group decision-making should support both types of group interaction by (i) maintaining Input/Output compatibility (e.g., data flows) between the individual model component and the group model component, and (ii) allowing multitasking. In a multiple criteria group decision-making framework, the single user MCDM stored in the individual model base should be independent from each other, but logically interrelated with the group MCDM (e.g., outputs from single user MCDM become inputs to group decision model). Also, each group member can concurrently run various decision models and, if necessary, communications routines.

5.2 TECHNIQUES OF AGGREGATION OF PREFERENCES FOR GROUP DECISION SUPPORT

This section discusses some of the most well known techniques of aggregation of preferences. The latter can be classified as content-oriented methods and can be stored in the group model base.

There are at least three reasons that explain the necessity of having more than one group decision technique. First, there are two different forms of output usually found in single user MCDM. The first type of output is the matrix of outranking relations (e.g., ELECTRE I). The second type of output – which is by far the most common – is represented by a vector of ordinal or cardinal ranking (e.g., AHP) of preferences. The group algorithm should support these two types of individual outputs.

Second, none of the techniques of aggregation of preferences currently known in the literature can satisfy all five conditions imposed by Arrow's Impossibility Theorem (Arrow, 1963) (see section 3.1.1). The combination of various techniques could at least be used as an attempt to reduce the impact of the lack of a perfect group technique.

Finally, the combination of decision techniques can increase the chances of reaching a consensus, or can at least constitute a richer basis for bargaining and negotiation.

In addition to the majority vote, ten algorithms for aggregating individual preferences are often discussed in the management science literature. These techniques operate under the following assumptions:

(1)   All participants of the group problem solving share the same set of alternatives, but not necessarily the same set of evaluation criteria.

(2)   Prior to the group decision-making process, each decision maker or group member must have performed his own assessment of preferences. The output of such analysis is a vector of normalized and cardinal ranking, a vector of ordinal ranking, or a vector of outranking relations performed on the alternatives.

Using the following definitions:

n = number of alternatives,

m = number of decision makers

a_i = alternative a_i (for $i = 1,...,n$)

r_{a_id} = cardinal ranking of alternative a_i

(for i = 1,...,n) by decision maker d

(for d = 1,...,m) where $\sum r_{a_i}$ = 1 for each d.

c_{a_id} = ordinal ranking of alternative a_i

(for i = 1,...,n) by decision maker d
(for d = 1,...,m)

$o_{a_ia_kd}$ = outranking relation

(= 1) indicating that a_i outranks a_k (for i,k = 1,...,n)
by decision maker d(for d = 1,...,m);
(= 0) indicating that there is no outranking relation.

the following aggregation of preferences techniques can be performed.

(1) The Min-Max Principle

The safest and unquestioned principle in dealing with group problem solving is the min-max concept in game theory (von Neumann and Morgenstern, 1953). Applied to the concordance/discordance concept in ELECTRE, a_i 'collectively' outranks a_k when its lowest concordance and its highest discordance given by the group satisfy the outranking condition sanctioned by the highest concordance threshold and the lowest discordance threshold also given by the group.

The group concordance index, $C^G_{a_ia_k}$, the group discordance index, $D^G_{a_ia_k}$, the group concordance threshold, p^G, and the group discordance threshold, q^G can be respectively computed as follows to identify collectively non-dominated alternative(s):

$$C^G_{a_ia_k} = \min\ [\ c_{a_ia_kd}\ |\ d=1,...,u]$$

$$D^G_{a_ia_k} = \max\ [\ d_{a_ia_kd}\ |\ d=1,...,u]$$

$$p^G = \max\ [\quad p_d\ |\ d=1,...,u]$$

$$q^G = \min\ [\quad q_d\ |\ d=1,...,u]$$

In a cooperative decision-making environment, the minimum of concordance/maximum of discordance concept (as illustrated in Section 4.2.) often helps reduce the number of non-dominated alternatives found in individual analyses to a smaller set of – or even to a unique-collective nondominated alternative(s).

However, the min-max principle works only when individual opinions are not extreme, and/or the number of alternatives is sufficiently large to generate consensus – as it does to a group version of UTA, an additive utility method (Shakun, 1984). Each group member can block a decision by setting a low discordance threshold (q) or by disagreeing completely in the evaluation of the alternatives (i.e., empty consensus set).

(2) The Sums-of-the-Outranking-Relations Principle

This technique is derived from the sum-of-the-ranks technique found in the literature of aggregation of preferences. Formally, it can be expressed as follows:

$$\text{Max}\left[\sum_{d=1}^{u} \sum_{a_i \neq a_k}^{n} O_{a_i a_k d}\right]$$

This technique should be used only with extreme care. Experience with this technique has shown that the idea of selecting the alternative that has the highest number of outranking relations works fine only when the number of alternatives are small.

(3) Pairwise Comparison Majority Rule

The Condorcet principle is based on a pairwise comparison scheme. It suggests that the alternative that receives a majority of votes against every other candidate should be elected:

$$\text{Max} \left[\sum_{d=1}^{u} \sum_{i=1 | a_i > a_k}^{n} O_{a_i a_k d} \right]$$

An example with three decision makers and three alternatives, with a_3 as the elected alternative, is given below.

Ordinal Ranking				Outranking Relations				
Rank	DM$_1$	DM$_2$	DM$_3$	Alt.	a_1	a_2	a_3	Sums of the Relations
1	a_1	a_3	a_3	a_1	–	2	1	3
2	a_2	a_1	a_2	a_2	1	–	1	2
3	a_3	a_2	a_1	a_3	2	2	–	4 <-Max

(4) Agenda Setting Rule

The 'agenda setting' or sequential pairwise comparison (Black, 1958) favors the candidate that enters last in the comparison process. Thus, according to this rule, a_3 should be elected in the example shown below:

Ordinal Ranking				Outranking Relations				
Rank	DM$_1$	DM$_2$	DM$_3$	Alt.	a_1	a_2	a_3	Sums of the Relations
1	a_1	a_2	a_3	a_1	–	2	1	3
2	a_2	a_3	a_1	a_2	1	–	2	3
3	a_3	a_1	a_2	a_3	2	1	–	3

(5) Sums-of-the-Ranks Rule

The sums-of-the-ranks rule (Borda, 1781) can be defined as follows:

$$\text{Min}\left[\sum_{d=1}^{u} \sum_{i=1}^{n} r_{a_i d}\right]$$

where $r_{a_i d}$ is the rank assigned by decision maker d to alternative a_i. The example below illustrates this rule.

Alternative	DM$_1$	DM$_2$	DM$_3$	Sums-of-the-Ranks
a_1	4	4	2	10
a_2	1	1	3	5 <–Min
a_3	2	2	4	8
a_4	3	3	1	7

Due to its computational simplicity this technique is widely used to determine consensus ranking. Note that the averages-of-the-ranks rule yields the same results. However, when there are ties, the results are different.

(6) The Additive Ranking

The additive ranking applies when individual assessments of alternatives are expressed in cardinal values. A group evaluation of an alternative is the arithmetic mean of the rankings made by all group members. Due to its simplicity, the additive ranking approach remains one of the most frequently used technique of aggregation of preferences:

$$r_{a_i}^G = \frac{\sum\limits_{d=1}^{u} r_{a_i d}}{u}$$

(7) The Multiplicative Ranking

This method aims to give each group member more impact on the group outcome. A group evaluation of an alternative is the product of the rankings made by all group members raised to the power of u decision makers. The multiplicative effect allows an individual to impose his/her veto:

$$r_{a_i}^G = \sqrt[u]{\prod_{d=1}^{u} r_{a_i d}}$$

(8) The Minimum Variance Method

The Minimum-Variance Method (Cook and Seiford, 1982) is an extension of the sums-of-the-ranks rule. When there are ties in ranking alternatives, this statistical algorithm searches for an estimated ranking that is close to the true ranking of the alternatives. More formally, the purpose of the Minimum-Variance method is to estimate the 'mean ranking', b_{a_i} (i=1,...,n), which minimizes:

$$\text{Min}\left[\sum_{i=1}^{n} (r_{a_i} - b_{a_i})^2\right]$$

where b_{a_i} is the average of the ranks of an alternative $\left(b_{a_i} = \frac{1}{m}\sum_{i=1}^{u} r_{a_i}\right)$

The example shown below illustrates the difference between the Borda rule and the M-V method with five decision makers and five alternatives:

Alt.	DM_1	DM_2	DM_3	DM_4	DM_5	Sums of the Ranks	Ranks	M-V Estimation	Ranks
a_1	2	1	2	1	3	9	2nd	1.5	1st
a_2	3	3	4	4	2	16	3rd	3.0	3rd
a_3	5	4	5	3	5	22	5th	4.5	4th
a_4	1	2	1	2	1	7	1st	1.5	1st
a_5	4	5	3	5	4	21	4th	4.5	4th

(9) Compromise Ranking Rule

The compromise ranking rule that has its roots in transportation algorithms (Zeleny, 1982), attempts to minimize individual ranking differences. Formally, the ranking can be computed as follows:

$$\text{Min}\left[\sum_{i=1}^{n} \sum_{d=1}^{u} (r_{a_i d} - RM) \right]$$

where RM is the rank median $\left(RM = \frac{m+1}{2} \right)$. In the example shown below, the compromise ranking rule yields a group ranking vector [2,1,3], suggesting a_2 to be the elected alternative.

Rank	DM_1	DM_2	DM_3	Alt.	a_1	a_2	a_3	$r_{a_i d}$ - RM
1	a_1	a_3	a_2	a_1	–	2	1	2
2	a_2	a_1	a_3	a_2	1	–	1	1<– Min
3	a_3	a_2	a_1	a_3	2	2	–	3

(10) Weighted Majority Rule

This rule is based on the observation that the participants of a group may not carry the same weight in the decision-making process. This can be due to the differences in decisional skills, problem knowledge and expertise, or hierarchical power in organizations. Thus, a vector of weights must be included in the aggregation of preferences or rankings. Fishburn and Gehrlein (1977), Nitzan and Paroush (1983) provide formal proofs of this rule.

In a decision situation that consists of five members, Nitzan and Paroush (1983) enumerate seven possible vector of weights:

(i)   The Expert Rule (1,0,0,0,0): The decision depends entirely on the most qualified decision maker;

(ii)   Simple Majority Rule (1,1,1,1,1): The decision makers share the same weight;

(iii)   Restricted Simple Majority Rule (1,1,1,0,0): Only the votes of the most competent decision makers are considered;

(iv)   Restricted Simple Majority Rule with a Tie-Breaking Chairman (2,1,1,0,0): If the restricted simple majority rule leads to a tie, the most competent decision makers make the final choice;

(v)   Nearly Simple Majority Rule I (2,2,1,1,1): All decision makers' votes are considered. However, the most able decision makers, despite their minority, are decisive;

(vi)   Nearly Simple Majority Rule II (3,2,2,1,1): This is similar to the previous definition, with a distinction between highly competent, competent, and moderately competent decision makers;

(vii) The Nearly Expert Rule (3,1,1,1,1): This is similar to the expert rule. However, the expert shares some of his decisional power.

Note that this rule must be used either with the additive ranking or the multiplicative ranking.

5.3 CONSENSUS SEEKING ALGORITHM IN GROUP DECISION SUPPORT

If no non-dominated alternative can be reached in the first round of the group MCDM, negotiations become necessary to analyze, and possibly resolve, individual differences. This section proposes an algorithm for supporting decision makers to analyze individual differences when techniques of aggregation of preferences fail to identify unanimity. The *Negotiable Alternative Identifier (NAI)* is presented below. It is based on a three-step concept, i.e., the expansion/ contraction/intersection mechanism (Bui, 1985b). A real-life application of this algorithm is described in Bui and Shakum (1987).

5.3.1 The Expansion/Contraction/Intersection Concept

Starting with individual and cardinal rankings of alternatives, the proposed algorithm is motivated by the following observations. First, in order to improve the chance of reaching consensus, the decision makers should exhibit some flexibility regarding their individual assessment of preferences. Second, they should be able to identify exchangeable or negotiable alternatives.

The NAI algorithm attempts to help the decision makers measure their degree of flexibility regarding their individual assessment of preferences by examining their *distribution of preferences* among alternatives. It is based on the observation that cardinal ranking of alternatives is a function of two factors.

First, the total number of alternatives being evaluated can affect the intensity of preferences. Often, the greater the number of alternatives, the weaker the relative importance of the alternatives. Second, the distribution of marginal difference among alternatives is rarely uniform. For example, some alternatives share close evaluation (e.g., A_1 and A_2 with respective score of 33% and 32%); Furthermore, some others score significant marginal difference (e.g., A_3 and A_4 respectively with 25% and 10%).

NAI is characterized by a triple operation: expansion, contraction and intersection. The objective of the first operation is to reassess individual preferences by locating possible areas of compromise. In effect, when a decision maker first attempts to establish an order of preferences, his analysis often results in a ranking of the alternatives subject to evaluation. He would then logically choose the alternative that is ranked first in the vector of preferences. However, unless the chosen alternative obviously outranks its counterparts, there is no reason why the next ranked alternative could not be considered as a comparatively acceptable solution. The same argument is also applicable for the second and third alternatives, the third and fourth alternatives, etc.

The NAI algorithm uses differential techniques to group ranked alternatives into two classes of preferences: the preferred and the least preferred sets of alternatives. Within each class, negligible differences in preferences between alternatives would increase the confidence of the decision makers not to discriminate them. As a consequence, it would make it easier for the decision maker to trade them. In other words, grouping alternatives that share close evaluation corresponds to expanding the preference space(s) of the decision maker from one best alternative to a set of more or less equally preferred alternatives.

The *contraction* operation constitutes the second phase of the NAI algorithm. Given a subset of comparatively satisfactory alternatives obtained from the expansion mapping, the second operation attempts to identify those that might exhibit a stronger preferential distribution than others.

Based on observation of the preferred alternatives, there are some that seem to play a role of 'leader' and some others the role of 'follower'. This idea is similar to the phenomenon of leader-follower found in the market theory (Shubik, 1964). Therefore, if among the preferred alternatives, there *still* remains an unequal distribution of preferences, then, at least theoretically speaking, there must be an indicator that helps distinguish the most preferred from the preferred alternatives.

The third and last step is the *intersection* operation. It derives a collective solution(s) that is(are) acceptable to all group members. Consensus is reached when there is at least one alternative that appears in every group member's subset of the most preferred alternatives.

As a result, it is expected that a collective decision that may not be necessarily unanimous but is essentially acceptable by all can be suggested. Conversely, if the intersection operation fails to identify a collective solution, this could be seen as an early indicator suggesting that consensus seeking should be replaced by some form of conflict dissolution.

5.3.2 The Expansion/Contraction/Intersection Algorithm

As discussed earlier, the distribution of preferences among alternatives reflects the extent to which alternatives are related to each other. With alternatives expressed by cardinal preferences, a vector of ranking is sorted according to an order of decreasing importance. In other words, r_1 represents the relative preference of the most preferred alternative, and r_n the relative preference of the least preferred alternative. Given the vector r_i,

R_i can be defined as the cumulative preference that a decision maker gives to the first i alternative(s).

Then, the Structural Index of Preferences of alternatives, $SI_{d,j}$ can be defined as follows. For a decision maker d,

$$SI_{d,j} = \left(\frac{1}{j}\right) M$$

where:

$$M = \left(\frac{1}{j-1}\right) M_k$$

$$M_k = \left[\frac{\left(\frac{R_k}{k}\right)}{\left(\frac{R_j - R_k}{j-k}\right)} \right]$$

and where: j = 2,...,n; and k = 1,...,j - 1 are summation indexes.

In other words, M_k is the ratio between the cumulative preference per alternative assigned to better alternatives and that of the residual alternatives. M is an average value of M_k. The structural index $SI_{d,j}$ puts this average M on a per alternative basis.

The value of $SI_{d,j}$ is a function of the number of alternatives j, as well as the distribution of the decision maker's preferences r_i. Theoretically, $SI_{d,j}$ varies between 1/j (i.e., situation in which the decision maker is completely indifferent with regard to alternatives) and ∞ (i.e., maximum of 'disequilibrium' among distribution of preferences). Furthermore, one might argue that the closer the value of $SI_{d,j}$ to 1/j the easier for the decision maker to negotiate with other members of the group.

Conversely, the higher the value of $SI_{d,j}$, the smaller the degree of willingness or flexibility in negotiation.

Thus, from a consensus seeking point of view, it would pay to concentrate the analysis on the situation in which an individual decision maker shows strong preferences in favor of a small subset of alternatives.

Step 1: The Expansion Operation

Given a set of n ranked alternatives, the subset of preferred alternatives can be defined as the one composed by the top alternatives, say n*, that are clearly more preferred than the 'residual' alternatives, i.e., n - n*. The identification of the number of preferred alternatives n* as well as the rationale of the approach are described below:

(1) Define n - 1 subsets of alternatives: The first subset is composed of the first two alternatives (j=2). The second one is composed by the first three alternatives (j=3), etc. And the (n - 1)th subset is the entire set itself (j=n).

(2) For each subset of j alternatives, compute its structural index of preferences, $SI_{d,j}$, where j=2,...,n:

$$SI_{d,j} = \{SI_{d,2},..., SI_{d,n}\}$$

(3) The subset containing the most preferred alternatives is the one that has the lowest $SI_{d,j}$:

$$SI_{d,n*} = Min \{SI_{d,j}\}$$

where n* represents the first n alternatives that form the subset of the most preferred alternatives $(2 \leq n* \leq n)$.

The rationale of using the smallest $SI_{d,j}$ as the cut-off point can be justified by the observation that the lower the value of $SI_{d,j}$ the more uniform the distribution of preferences among alternatives. Thus, by choosing n^* that has the minimum value of $SI_{d,j}$ as the cut-off point, one can argue that the decision maker d has more or less evenly distributed his/her preferences among the n^* alternatives. In other words, numerical differences between n^* alternatives are not significant enough to assert that none of the alternatives is clearly worse than another to the extent that it should be discarded.

From a group problem solving point of view, a SI_{d,n^*} with a high value would indicate that the decision maker d has a strong and clear cut choice, and as a consequence, there may be little room left for concession making. On the other hand, a SI_{d,n^*} with a small value suggests that the decision maker d would exhibit some indifference among alternatives, and as a consequence, this would make it easier for him to trade among them.

Step 2: The Contraction Operation

The contraction operation can be performed by referring to a component of the definition of the structural index $SI_{d,j}$. In effect, the ratio M_k could be used to reflect the relative strength of the first alternatives to the residual alternatives. The idea here is to find out which subset of the preferred set does belong to the most preferred subset. Given n^* preferred alternatives, the identification of a second cut-off can be done by applying the following steps:

(1)   Define $n^* - 1$ subsets of alternatives in a bottom up manner: The first bottom subset is composed by the n^* alternatives minus the top one. The second bottom subset is composed by n^* alternatives minus the first two top alternatives; etc. And the $(n^* - 1)$th bottom subset contains only one alternative, the one just above the cut-off point for the preferred set.

(2)   Compute the arithmetic mean, $\overline{r_i}'$, of the cardinal preferences for each subset i´, where i´ = 1,...,n* - 1 corresponds respectively to the first to the (n* - 1)th bottom subset as defined in (1).

(3)   For i* = 1,...,n* - 1, compute the $C_{d,i*}$ preference ratio index as follows:

$$C_{d,i*} = \frac{r_{i*}}{\overline{r_i}'}$$

where r_{i*} is the cardinal preference for alternative i*, the last top alternative defining a cutoff point separating the bottom subset from the alternatives above.   Note in working with the n* alternatives in the preferred set that their cardinal preferences are renormalized so that their sum over the preferred set equals one.

(4)   Choose the second cutoff point i* by maximizing the $C_{d,i*}$ preference ratio, i.e., Max$\{C_{d,i*}\}$ for i* = 1,...,n* - 1.   The rationale for this is as follows. If $C_{d,i*}$ is large, then there is a big relative drop between the preference value r_{i*} of the alternative just above the cutoff point compared to the average preference $\overline{r_i}'$, of the alternatives in the subset below.   Thus, Max$\{C_{d,i*}\}$ is a good criterion for the subset of most preferred alternatives at the top of the preferred set.

        In other words, the alternatives that are situated above this second cutoff point are considered most preferred.   It is assumed that the decision maker would be reluctant to drop these alternatives out.   In a situation of complete indifference, all $C_{d,i*}$ = 1 are maximum and we would set i* = n*.

Step 3: The Intersection Operation

Given all individual subset of i* (most preferred) alternatives, an intersection operation can be performed to identify possible consensus solution(s). Similarly, a intersection operation can be performed on individual subsets of n* (preferred) alternatives. This would provide a set of alternatives subject to eventual negotiations.

5.3.3   An Example

The example illustrated below is a simplified description of an actual application of NAI. It particularly demonstrates the ability of the algorithm to enlarge the decision space, and consequently, reduce potential frustration caused by individual differences.

Table 5.1 exhibits the cardinal rankings of a hypothetical married couple who are searching for a vacation site. Six alternatives are considered: San Francisco, Grand Canyon, Hawaii, New York, Japan and Europe. The individual rankings are obtained from a cooperative multiple criteria group DSS using the Analytic Hierarchy Method. For comparison purposes, Table 5.2 reproduces the group results computed according to four different types of aggregation of preferences techniques: (i) sums of the ranks, (ii) additive ranking, (iii) multiplicative ranking, and (iv) pairwise comparison (see section 5.2).

It is worth noting that the four techniques of aggregation mentioned above do not lead to the same collective decision. More important is the fact that none of these techniques could reconcile the individual differences in selecting the 'best' individual outcome. If one of these techniques has to be adopted to sanction a group decision, two adverse situations could occur. First, one of the spouses whose individual decision does not concord with the 'collective' result, may simply decide to keep his/her preferences unchanged. Such a decision naturally leads to an impasse. On the other hand, the spouse may reluctantly conform with the aggregation of preferences outcome. Such an obligation could later on plant some seeds of dissonance and create low morale in future group problem solving.

The results of the NAI algorithm are presented in Tables 5.3 and 5.4. The expansion and contraction operations suggest that the wife was in fact not firmly committed to the first alternative (e.g., San Francisco). Her distribution of preferences would indicate that the next four alternatives could also be considered. On the other hand, NAI shows a stronger preference pattern in the husband's decision. In effect, the subset of most preferred alternatives is reduced to two alternatives. The intersection operation on the spouses' sets of the preferred alternatives suggests that Hawaii would be the consensus.

VACATION SITE	CARDINAL RANKING		ORDINAL RANKING	
	Husband	Wife	Husband	Wife
San Francisco	.11	.40	5	1
Grand Canyon	.19	.20	3	2
Hawaii	.22	.17	2	3
New York	.18	.15	4	4
Japan	.05	.06	6	5
Europe	.25	.02	1	6

Table 5.1. Examples of Individual Rankings

VACATION SITE	RULE 1	RULE 2	RULE 3	RULE 4
San Francisco	6	.26*	.21*	6
Grand Canyon	5*	.19	.19	7*
Hawaii	5*	.19	.19	7*
New York	8	.17	.16	4
Japan	11	.06	.05	1
Europe	7	.14	.07	5

Legend:
   Rule 1 : Minimize sums of the ranks
   Rule 2 : Maximize additive ranking
   Rule 3 : Maximize multiplicative ranking
   Rule 4 : Pairwise Comparison (max.)
   An * indicates the optimal solution

Table 5.2. Results Obtained From the Techniques of Aggregation of Preferences

HUSBAND

ALTERNATIVE	$SI_{d,n}$	$C_{d,i}$
Europe	—	—
Hawaii	.56	.62*
Grand Canyon	.41	.41
New York	.31*	.48
San Francisco	.32	—
Japan	.39	—

WIFE

ALTERNATIVE	$SI_{d,n}$	$C_{d,i}$
Europe	—	—
Hawaii	1.00	.88
Grand Canyon	.65	.57
New York	.49*	.96*
San Francisco	.57	—
Japan	.84	—

Table 5.3.   The NAI Results for the Vacation Example

HUSBAND	WIFE
EXPANSION OPERATION:	
Europe	San Francisco
Hawaii	Grand Canyon
Grand Canyon	Hawaii
New York	New York
CONTRACTION OPERATION:	
Europe	San Francisco
Hawaii	Grand Canyon
New York	Hawaii
INTERSECTION OPERATION:	
• from subsets of preferred alternatives:	
Hawaii	
New York	
• from subsets of most preferred alternatives	
Hawaii	

Table 5.4. The NAI Results (Continued)

In summary, the expansion/contraction mappings provide some basis for understanding the extent to which a decision maker is committed to his/her assessment of preferences. Experience has often shown that decision makers are more flexible than the outcomes of some decision techniques would advocate. The indexes of distribution of preferences discussed in this paper could be used to interpret the degree of flexibility of the decision makers. The discovery and analysis of this margin of flexibility would make it easier for the decision makers to safely accept, and more important, to heartily endorse the collective decision outcome.

Furthermore, if the expansion/contraction/intersection operations still lead to a collective impasse (i.e., empty set), the proposed algorithm would at least indicate that some radical solutions should be taken to reach some consensus. These solutions would include open discussion of the members' distribution of preferences, modification of the decision space, or generation of additional alternatives (see section 4.3.2).

5.4 PROCESS-ORIENTED GROUP DECISION TECHNIQUES

The purpose of process-oriented models is to promote non-quantified group problem solving. These models include the Delphi method and computerized conferencing system. The Delphi method has proven successful in resolving problems that involve a large number of decision makers marked by heterogeneity or lack of shared norms for interaction (Mitroff and Turoff, 1975; Scheele, 1975; Linstone and Turoff, 1975). The 'computerization' of this technique is expected to increase the efficiency of the decision-making process (i.e., speed and low cost of processing information), and the quality of the decision outcomes (i.e., media that help the group focus its efforts) (Hiltz and Turoff, 1978)).

5.4.1 Interacting, Nominal and Delphi Processes

The first and most widely used process-oriented approach is the interacting group method in which collective decision making occurs within a face-to-face setting and all communication takes place between group members with minimal restraints imposed (Delbecq, 1968). The resultant decision outcome is reached after a process of (i) unstructured group discussion for gaining and merging group member's ideas, and (ii) majority voting on priorities by hand count.

The nominal group technique is a structured group meeting in which decision makers perform in the proximity of others but do not interact in an explicit or verbal way for a specified period of time. Each individual is tasked with the writing of ideas on a notepad. At the completion of the allotted time period, each group member, in a round-robin fashion, contributes one idea from his or her tabulation to be documented by a recorder. The round-robin is in effect until no further ideas are presented, and then a spontaneous discussion occurs among the group. As a final step, voting by all the members is conducted, with the group decision being the aggregated or pooled outcome of the members' votes. The method of group decision making is recapitulated in the following order (Van de Ven, 1974):

(i)   Silent generation of ideas in writing;

(ii)   Recorded round-robin feedback from each member for presentation of ideas to the group;

(iii)   Discussion of recorded ideas to evaluate information; and

(iv)   Silent individual voting on priorities.

The Delphi method is a much more elaborate process. Participants in the Delphi process are physically separated and do not meet as a group for decision-making. This procedure is one way of seeking and finally aggregating group judgments on a particular issue through a set of carefully designed questionnaires. To conduct the Delphi process, at least two separate groups of individuals and at least four roles or functions for individual groups are required. There is a user body in which the individuals are expecting a product from the exercise which is useful to their purposes. A design and monitor team, which may be separate groups, designs the initial questionnaire, summarizes the returns, and re-designs the subsequent questionnaires. The respondent group is chosen to respond to the questionnaires and may sometimes be the user group or a subset of the respondent group.

The sequence of decision making in the Delphi process occurs in the following order:

(i) Independent generation of ideas by responding to the first questionnaire by the respondent group;

(ii) Construction of synopsis and feedback of the replies to the first questionnaire by the design and monitoring team ;

(iii) Design a subsequent questionnaire through detached voting on ideas by a rank order procedure from a previous questionnaire; and

(iv) Final aggregation and feedback with assessment of priorities.

The differences between interacting, nominal, and Delphi processes are described by Van de Ven (1974) in Table 5.5. These

	Interacting or F-T-F Mode	Nominal Group Technique	Delphi Technique
Method of Problem Solving	Person-centered	Problem-centered	Problem-centered
Methodology	Unstructured Group Meeting	Structured Meeting	Structure Questionnaire
Role Orientation	Reactive Short Problem	Balanced Focus on Social Maintenance and Task Role	Task Instrumental Focus
Search Behavior	Socio-emotional Group Maintenance	Pro-active, Extended Search	Pro-active, Controlled Problem
Normative Behavior	Conformity Pressures	Tolerance for Non-conformity	Freedom not to Conform
Attitude towards Tasks Problem	Low Task Motivation	High Task Motivation	Withdrawn Task Motivation
Member Participation	Member Dominance	Member Equality	Respondent Equality
Relative Quantity of Ideas	Low	Higher	High
Quality of Ideas	Low, Generalization	Higher Quality	High Quality, High Specificity
Decision Closure	High Lack of Closure	Lower Lack of Closure	Low Lack of Disclosure

Table 5.5. Differences between Face-to-Face metting, Nominal
Group Technique and Delphi

characteristics are based upon analysis of evaluations of leaders and group participants of various organizations.

5.4.2 Computerized Conferencing System and Electronic Mail

Computerized conferencing systems and electronic mail allow the decision makers to collectively or individually address unstructured or informal opinions.

The Computerized Conferencing System (CCS) is a written form of communication in which participants send or receive messages often in the privacy of their own workstation. The advantages of CCS are that it allows the participants to access to the system at their convenience and gives them the time to reflect on solutions and the possibility to exchange technical information (Johansen et al., 1979). Unlike CCS that is accessible to every member of the group, the electronic mail allows the decision makers to individually send and receive messages.

5.5 TOWARDS AN INTEGRATED MCDM MODEL BASE

In a multiple criteria *individual* decision-making environment, the use of a single MCDM often appears sufficient. Familiarity, experience, and subjective preference to a particular MCDM make it less appealing for the decision maker to refer to many MCDM. However, the context of group problem solving would argue for a integrated MCDM system. The purposes of the latter are (i) to support a wide variety of multiple criteria decision-making situations, (ii) to partially resolve the problems of information searches, and (iii) to provide a framework for division of decision-making tasks among members of the decision group.

5.5.1   Necessity to Support a Wide Range of Decision Situations

Roy (1978) distinguishes three types of MCDM according to the type of decision-making they support: MCDM for selection, MCDM for ranking and, MCDM for sorting. Thus, from a methodological perspective, the use of a selection-type MCDM (for example, the outranking relation concept of the ELECTRE 1 method (Roy, 1968)) is only appropriate when, from a given set of alternatives, only one is to be selected. If more than one alternative must be selected, the second and subsequent choice might not necessarily be non-dominated (Starr and Zeleny, 1977). Moreover, this same concept does not appropriately support the ranking of alternatives. Recourse to another MCDM method would be more desirable.

In addition, the nature and the quality of information that the decision makers can input into a MCDM also influence the selection of a particular MCDM method. For illustrative purposes, when only the expertise of the decision makers can be relied upon for a decision problem, the Analytic Hierarchy Method or ELECTRE 1 could be adopted since these methods do not require very accurate or objective information. However, when the decision maker possesses more information than AHP or ELECTRE would require, MCDM that provide a more precise, cardinal measurement of preferences can be employed, e.g., Multi-attribute Utility Theory methods (Keeny, 1976; Wendell, 1979; Shenoy, 1980, Moskowitz et al., 1981, or the Additive Utility Methods (UTA) (Jacquet-Lagreze and Siskos, 1982).

In sum, because of the unpredictable model requirements of a group problem solving situation, it would make a great deal of sense to provide the users with a set of decision models that could resolve the most common types of decision problems. Nevertheless, from a systems design point of view, it would be neither possible nor desirable for a GDSS to include all existing MCDM models. Rather, it would be more realistic and manageable to integrate a small set of models that (i) cover three basic decision situations, i.e., selection, ranking, sorting, (ii) represent current methodologies in MCDM and group decision-making, and, (iii) are relatively easy for the decision makers to use.

5.5.2   Economics of Information Searches

One of the most frequent obstacles found in decision-making is the unavailability of raw information necessary to assess the decision situation. First, the process of acquisition of information is time consuming and costly. Second, even if the decision makers can afford to spend a great deal of resources for information search, some pieces of information may still be unavailable, and keep preventing the use of decision models that require them (Stigler, 1961). It would thus be useful for a DSS to help decision makers minimize the number of information searches, given a desired decision outcome.

For any MCDM, regardless of its underlying methodology, the minimum number of information required is equal to the number of alternatives times the number of attributes or evaluation criteria. For example, selecting a house among a hundred houses based on ten evaluation criteria would require at least 1000 information searches. In particular, ELECTRE I requires at least 1010 searches, and AHP, 4995 searches in this situation.

The hypothetical example shown in Figure 5.1 demonstrates that a combined and sequential use of UTA and ELECTRE can reduce the number of information search as by more than half if compared to the use of ELECTRE I alone, or by a factor of 10 if compared to the use of UTA alone. In general, the exact number of searches saved depends on the nature of the problem and the MCDM adopted.

An integrated and unified MCDM system could not only reduce the *cost of information searches* but also may make it possible to overcome the *unavailability of information*.

STEP	ACTION(S)	MCDM USED	NUMBER OF SEARCHES
0	100 alternatives, 10 criteria	---	---
1	Among the 10 initial evaluation criteria, find the 2 most important ones	AHP	45**
2	Sort 100 alternatives according to the 2 criteria found in Step 2. Suppose that 30 non-dominated alternatives are found with ELECTRE	ELECTRE	200***
3	Choose the best alternatives among 30 non-dominated alternatives found in Step 2, according to the remaining 8 evaluation criteria	ELECTRE	240***
	Total number of information searches using combined MCDM		485

Figure 5.1. Reducing the Number of Information Searches using Successive MCDMs

5.5.3   Division of Decision-Making Tasks

In addition to the reduction of information searches, the possibility to sequentially combine methods for problem solving would make it easier to integrate the DSS into group or organizational decision situations. In fact, decision makers who participate to a group problem solving often share different responsibilities and retain different levels of expertise or power (Galbraith, 1967, 1973). They also perform decision-making sequentially in that a decision outcome of a member is the decision input of other member(s) of the group (Cyert and March, 1963). Under such circumstances, the performance of the group decision-making depends on the (1) availability of various decision techniques potentially needed for each member of the group, and (2) an appropriate combination of techniques (Thompson, 1967).

Figure 5.2 illustrates the capability of a unified MCDM system to support division of decision-making tasks. This example is a modified and simplified version of a real application of MCDM to help a multinational firm assess its acquisition strategies (Pasquier et al., 1981). The top management staff first assessed its corporate objectives by using the AHP method which does not require exact and quantified information. Based on this prioritization of objectives, the top management staff ran ELECTRE I to reduce the number of alternatives. Technical executives then used the MAUT method to perform detailed and technical evaluation of the new set of alternatives. The UTA method was performed next to explore new possibilities.

5.6 TOWARDS KNOWLEDGE-BASED MODEL MANAGEMENT SYSTEMS FOR MCDM

Attempts to integrate MCDM under a unified system cannot be done without generating another problem. In effect, the presence of large model

83

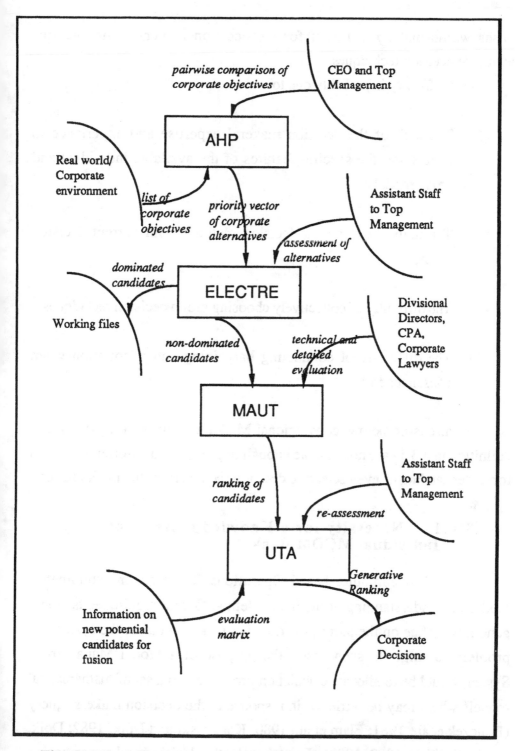

Figure 5.2. A Data Flow Diagram showing an Organizational Sequential Decision Making using MCDMs

bases would make it difficult for the decision makers to use various available decision techniques.

This difficulty is probably due to:

(1) The lack of the decision makers' expertise and experience to understand the specific features of the available individual and group models;

(2) The inability to match decision methods with current decision needs;

(3) The difficulty of collectively choosing group decision techniques.

(4) The difficulty of conducting bargaining and negotiation when consensus fails.

As discussed below, conventional Model Management Systems (see definition in 3.3.1) are not flexible enough to provide a user-oriented milieu for understanding or even selecting decision models from the model banks.

5.6.1 Necessity for a Knowledge Base for Individual MCDM Bank

With computer-based Operations Research or econometric models, an understanding of the Input-Method-Output requirements would generally suffice on the part of the decision maker to utilize the system for problem solving. In such cases, the purpose of a Model Management System would be to allocate calculation procedures to a set of mathematical models which may be retrieved in response to the decision makers' query (Bonczek et al., 1981; Elam et al., 1980; Konsynski and Dolk, 1982; Dolk, 1983; Blanning, 1982, 1983). For example, the decision maker can access a MCDM by simply writing a clause such as:

MCDM (INPUT:NA, NC, W, MC; OUTPUT: OR)

where NA, NC, W and MC are respectively the number of alternatives, number of criteria, vector of weights and matrix of evaluation of alternatives with respect to criteria. These inputs constitute the minimal information for a MCDM to compute an Ordering Ranking (OR) of alternatives. If there are *many* MCDM that can perform the same ranking problem using the same inputs (e.g., AHP and MAUT), additional information is required to determine a unique MCDM (e.g., AHP or MAUT).

The nature of information (i.e., quantitative or qualitative), the quality of information (i.e., complete or incomplete), the size of alternatives and criteria (i.e., large or small number), the extent to which the decision makers need to exchange information of the MCDM technique adopted, the type of group decision interaction (i.e., pooled-interdependent or sequential interdependent), the ability and experience of the decision makers' to cope with MCDM algorithms are only some of the factors that could be considered when selecting a MCDM.

One way to approach the problem would be to create a decision table such as the one shown in Table 5.6. Such an approach suffers, however, from rigidity in understanding, inserting, and controlling the decision rules. Moreover, the assessment of the selection factors relies much on the knowledge or expertise of one or many human MCDM experts or consultants rather than on a set of well-defined and certain rules (Roy, 1976). It would thus be useful to store some of this evolving knowledge in the MMS for MCDM.

MCDM SELECTION CRITERIA: IF			
Number of Alternatives (many?)	N	Y	Y
Number of Criteria (many?)	N	–	–
Nature of Information (quantifiable?)	N	Y	–
Quality of Information (complete?)	N	Y	N
Form of Group Interaction (sequential?)	–	Y	–
DM's Knowledge (familiarity with MCDM?)	–	Y	Y
ACTION: THEN			
Analytical Hierarchy Process	X		
Multi-attribute Additive Utility		X	
Electre III			X

Table 5.6 : An Example of Decision Table for Selecting a MCDM that Ranks Alternatives

5.6.2 Necessity for a Knowledge Base for Group Decision Techniques

The function of a Model Management System (MMS) for group decision techniques is twofold. First, the MMS has to find the group techniques that match the type of outputs sent from single user MCDM methods. For instance, the min-max principle or the sums of the outranking relations are the algorithms that could be used with the ELECTRE I method. This is relatively easy to do considering the homogeneity of output forms, mostly in the form of cardinal or ordinal rankings.

The second function consists of identifying to the users the most appropriate group decision technique(s). This function is substantially more important and difficult to perform because of the inherent methodological difficulty of group aggregation techniques. In effect, none of the existing aggregation algorithms is theoretically trouble-free. For example, the Min-Max principle is the closest to Arrow's condition of social choice, but leads easily to an empty set of collective choice (see section 3.1.1). Also, the use of the Condorcet rule (see section 3.1.1) may lead to the 'paradox of voting' characterized by the violation of the transitivity assumption (e.g., aPb, bPc and cPa). If such a situation occurred, the replacement of the Condorcet rule by the sums of the ranks principle (see section 5.2) could resolve the problem. Unfortunately, the sums-of-the-ranks principle may also give undesirable outcomes. The elimination of an alternative can lead to an unexpected change of the ranking of the remaining candidates. (This phenomenon is also known in the literature as 'Dependence on Irrelevant Alternatives').

Under these circumstances, it would be desirable to have a knowledge-based MMS that helps the group agree upon a collective choice principle that will in turn help identify the most satisfactory technique. For example, 'If the elected alternative must satisfy every individual member of the group, the Min-Max should be chosen'.

5.6.3 Necessity for a Knowledge Base for Negotiation Support

Section 4.3.2 discussed various mediation functions that a GDSS should provide. These functions include techniques to generate issues or alternatives and submit them to the group members for examination. However, this practice is not trouble-free. If issues are of differential importance, which one should be addressed first? As a point of departure, one might argue that the most important decision issue should have priority. Once it is resolved, the remaining ones will be easier to treat.

However, what happens if early efforts to resolve major differences fail? Likely, this makes the resolution of the remaining issues more difficult. In contrast, one might support the approach of resolving easy issues first. Since they are of minor importance, they are easier to trade off. In turn, their resolution creates a favorable climate for further consensus seeking. Again, it is not warranted that minor issues always be resolved. Further, if they are resolved, there will be fewer possibilities to trade off when group members start negotiating central points.

While it is almost impossible to model the optimal profile of a negotiation process, there are some guidelines derived from empirical studies of successful negotiation (e.g., Ilich, 1980). Also, there are 'rules of thumb' that can be learned from past experience. Thus, it would be useful to have an evolving knowledge base that gradually records rules, facts or principles, and an inference engine that couples these elements to provide some mediation guidelines.

SUMMARY

In group decision-making situations, this chapter proposed the design of a model component that consists of an intertwining of content-oriented methods with process-oriented methods. Content-oriented methods include techniques of aggregation of preferences and consensus seeking algorithms. While the former helps sanction group results, the latter searches for areas of compromise. Process-oriented methods range from free-format electronic mail to structured communications such as the Nominal Group Technique and the Delphi method. To support the intertwining of approaches, group DSS should provide concurrent use of various decision methods and intelligent model management systems.

In the MCDM context, this chapter elaborated a unified framework for building generalized multiple criteria DSS. A DSS that integrates various

MCDM can support a wide range of multiple decision situations, reduce the amount of information needed for MCDM inputs, and allow division of decision-making tasks.

6. DESIGN ISSUES FOR THE GDSS DIALOGUE COMPONENT

Recent DSS literature often views the problems of 'user interface' as issues related to various communications aspects between a computer user and the computer including hardware and software. For instance, Sprague and Carlson (1982) propose the ROMC (i.e., Representations, Operations, Memory, Controls) approach to analyze and design an appropriate DSS man-machine interface. However, in a computer-based group problem solving, the machine is no longer an end-node. Rather, it becomes an intermediary in the man-machine-man interface. Thus, studies that have so far concentrated solely on the ergonomics, effectiveness and psychological factors of the man-machine interaction (e.g., see Shneiderman, 1986), should be expanded to the man-to-man interaction via computer interfaces. This chapter briefly reviews some common profiles of current GDSS and discusses two major issues in this man-machine-man interface.

6.1 I/O TECHNOLOGY FOR GDSS

The interface characteristics of current GDSS has been dictated by progress made in Input/Output technology. Touchscreen technique, windowing and visual interface are the most common interface tools adopted by GDSS builders. For example, Gray (1987) built an electronic-based voting system that used the touch-screen technique that allows the user to see and point at the computer screen to interact with the GDSS. This I/O mode removes the burden of learning and remembering cryptic or difficult command structures. By reducing the group member's I/O effort to recognition, not recall, it is expected that group members would focus more on the group decision task.

A number of GDSS, e.g., Co-oP, Touchstone, Colab, use windows. A window is a frame that provides to the user *a* view of the problem. Windows can be created to trigger dialogue with the user (i.e., dialogue box), alert the user in the event of an unusual or important situation such as notification of incoming electronic mail or error condition (i.e., alert box) or to control different defaults settings of the GDSS (i.e., control box). In some GDSS, multiple windows can be evoked to concurrently display various source of information and to eventually generate multiple processing tasks. Graphics or visual objects could be created to improve the effective use of windows. Some GDSS, such as the Macintosh-based Participant Construct System or decision room also utilize icons, and/or colorful graphics under a window-interface environment. It is expected that the design of GDSS will continue to be driven by the I/O technology. Big high-resolution screen displays and the integration of voice and video pictures with digital CRT displays will probably open new opportunities for designing effective GDSS interface. In the meantime, it is critical to highlight additional interface design guidelines for GDSS.

6.2 MAN-MACHINE INTERFACE AND GROUP INTERACTION

In a single user environment, a user interface of a DSS should (i) be transparent and consistent to make the system easy to learn, use and remember; (ii) be suitable for both novice and expert use; (iii) let the user have control of the system and feel competent in task performance; (iv) promote effective usage and better decision-making; (v) and be efficient in the use of system resources (Stohr and White, 1982; Schneiderman, 1986). Although these design principles should prevail in building GDSS, importance should be given more to the concept of ease-of-use and transparency.

As indicated in Chapter 2, MCDM-based DSS users are often decision makers who deal with strategic and ill-structured problems. It is reasonable to expect that (i) the frequency of GDSS use is low and, (ii) familiarity with computers is insignificant to none. Under such a decision environment, a comprehensive, structured and controlled interface, such as sequences of hierarchical menus or carefully designed queries, seems to be most appropriate in order to satisfy the five design principles mentioned above (e.g., Miller, 1977; Zmud, 1979; Schneider, 1982).

Moreover, specifications for information display in a group user interface system are expected to be much more stringent than in single user interface system. Due to the diversity of the group members' knowledge and backgrounds, and the need to reduce misunderstanding during group communication, the Input/Output formats for group decision techniques should be universally recognizable or at least understandable by every member of the group. It is expected that in a collective decision-making environment, the design of man-machine interaction should be as explicit as possible as the size of the group increases. In other words, not only does the user interface has to be easy to understand (i.e., WYSIWYG – What You See Is What You Get), it should also be easily understood and accepted by at least the majority of users (WYSIWIS – What You See Is What I See). As such, the user interface constitutes a basis for group members' dialogue and feedback.

Furthermore, when the group is small and homogeneous, the group DSS should be able – on the users' request – to transfer detailed information between decision makers (e.g., duplication of individual inputs, outputs, intermediate results). Conversely, when the group is large or heterogeneous, a minimal and standard form of group information should prevail (e.g., overall group ranking), at least in the first round of the group decision-making process.

In addition to the necessity of selecting suitable and if possible, favorable interfaces, the group interface system should be supplemented with user-interface tools that help the members perform various group decision activities. The latter include initiation (e.g., How does the group start the collective making process? Should the group elect a person that leads the discussion?); exchanging information (e.g., How can a member ask or share information?); analyzing group discussions or decision (e.g., How should the group interpret the results?); and consensus testing (e.g., What decision technique(s) should the group adopt – democratic vote or weighted majority rule?). The group DSS interface should be able to provide flexible 'Help' commands that clarify these tasks.

6.3 MAN-MACHINE-MAN INTERFACE: FORMAL VERSUS INFORMAL COMMUNICATIONS

According to Pye et al. (1973), the activities associated with the five types of group decision problems discussed in section 4.3.1 constitute a mixture of positive and negative reactions, problem solving attempts and 'questions'. Short et al. (1976) suggest that negative and positive reactions could be classed together as *person-oriented* communications since they reflect attitudes of one participant of the group toward another. Meanwhile, the search for information and problem-solving attempts could be classified as *non-person-oriented* communications since they are primarily concerned with the content of the decision problem.

Even if the conceptual distinction between person-oriented and non-person-oriented communication were trivial due to the ambiguity of human behavior, it could guide us in selecting suitable communication channels between individual DSS. Chapter 7 proposes a GDSS communications architecture that supports differentiation of these two interpersonal relationships.

Furthermore, Morley and Stephenson (1970, 1977) conducted various experiments to assess the effects of media on conflict resolution (see also section 3.3.2). Among other things, they all lead to the hypothesis that formal communication (e.g., official telephone conversation, written correspondence) places greater emphasis on the object of the discussion at the expense of the interpersonal exchange. Short (1974) found similar findings.

Although in need of replication with more sophisticated field studies, these findings suggest that one includes both formal and informal communication facilities in the Group DSS. Figures 6.1 and 6.2 are examples of interfaces, formal and informal communications, respectively.

The concept of formal communication leads to the idea of 'structuring' communication, as opposed to the idea that group processes should occur 'naturally'. The need to structure communication is primarily motivated by the increasing size of the group (also see section 6.1). As its size increases, the group becomes heterogeneous, loses control of its norms for interactions, and is prone to undesirable interpersonal influences. Among undesirable behaviors found in a group, one can recognize (i) the 'surveillance effect' (Asch, 1951) that pushes people to go along with the group rather than specify their own ideas, (ii) the individual lack of confidence when facing group pressure (Allen, 1970), and (iii) the 'leadership phenomenon' that prevents equal participation of opinion.

Thus, the design of structured communication interfaces – such as fill-in-the-form input/output formats – should (i) promote independent generation of ideas or judgments, (ii) enforce mechanisms for assuring equal opportunity to participate in the discussion, and (iii) provide organized feedback for group discussion.

Meanwhile, the identification of unstructured communication interfaces should fulfill some interpersonal communications needs that structured interfaces cannot provide. For instance, under a controlled

** GDSS-CCS MESSAGE CREATED ON 8-18-84 AT 19:20:23
** FROM: BROWN, PLANNING DIRECTOR
** TO: PLANNING TASK GROUP

Sales in Zone 4 have dropped regularly for the last 7 months.
Please answer to the questions below and return your comments
to me by August 25.

ADVERTISEMENT EFFORT	1 2 3 4 5
SALES EFFORT	1 2 3 4 5
PRICING POLICY	1 2 3 4 5
PRODUCT DIFFERENTIATION	1 2 3 4 5

(NOTE: 1:excellent., 2:good, 3:average 3:fair, 5:poor)

Figure 6.1. An Example of Formal Computer-based Communication

** GDSS-E-MAIL CREATED ON 8-18-84 AT 11:34:21
** FROM: MORRIS, GROUP MEMBER
** TO: OWENS, GROUP MEMBER

Jim:
I have an urgent meeting with a customer from New York. I
won't be able to attend the next meeting. However, please pick
up my spreadsheet program for the department budget from Gail.
If you think the template is useful for other members of the
group, please feel free to send them a copy via the net. See you.

P.S. I'd like a F-T-F meeting with you before we go and talk to
Fred.

**Figure 6.2. An Example of Informal Computer-based Communication
using Computer Conferencing**

environment, on-line and public notepad, electronic bulletin board or, electronic mail could enhance interpersonal interface.

SUMMARY

This chapter emphasized the importance of a GDSS interface that should unambiguously convey information across members of a decision group. Assuming a relatively low frequency of GDSS use, this chapter proposed the design of an explicit, structured and standard interface throughout the collective decision-making process.

Furthermore, the design of a GDSS should go beyond the man-machine boundaries. In fact, the DSS under group decision situations is itself an interface between users. This chapter suggested a double design strategy. First, a GDSS should provide both formal and informal man-machine-man interfaces to enhance information exchange within group members. Second, the GDSS should be designed in such a way that (i) it becomes favorable media for solving group problems, and (ii) it ensures that decision makers do not waste unnecessary resources in interpersonal exchange at the expense of a thorough discussion of the object of the group problem.

Implementing these two requirements, however, may lead to conflicting design strategies. A liberal and format-free communications policy favors information exchange, but could create superfluous group problems. Conversely, a restrictive and structured interface might seriously reduce the chance of breaking a group decision impasse. Determining an appropriate man-machine-man interface strategy requires understanding of a specific group decision problem as well as appreciation of particular communications norms among users. The design principle WYSIWIS (What You See Is What I See) should be understood as 'What You *should* see is what I see' appropriate to the group outcome. The next chapter proposes a framework to help group members define GDSS communications parameters that realistically reflect their particular interpersonal interface requirements.

7. COMMUNICATIONS DESIGN IN GDSS

Communications control in computer systems includes operations that enable data exchange to take place. In turn, communication protocols can be defined as a set of rules and formats permitting the control of communication between two stations (e.g., Puzman and Porizek, 1980). Studies on computer communications have benefited from an already numerous but still growing literature. Most of this work focuses, however, on the performance of data communication systems (e.g., access control, routing, congestion control, efficiency), rather than on the ability and requirements of the end-users or decision makers to analyze, specify and adjust these systems for domain-specific use.

From a GDSS standpoint, the analysis and design of communications support should go beyond the usual focus on technical issues of communications control such as network topology, network design, capacity and flow assignment, error detection, etc. In effect, establishing reliable and efficient communication can only be viewed as a prerequisite for supporting computer-based distributed group problem solving. A situation-dependent communication-driven GDSS not only has to indicate to individual DSS how to communicate, but how they should interact.

7.1 COMMUNICATIONS REQUIREMENTS IN GROUP DECISION-MAKING

In the context of a distributed group decision-making, the demands for information exchange are marked by certain characteristics that should be considered in the design of communications capabilities. These characteristics could be best expressed by the requirements of having information exchanges that are (i) format-transparent, (ii) either constrained or unconstrained, and (iii) evolving throughout the decision making phases.

7.1.1 Need for Format-Transparent Information Exchange

The demand for and/or generation of information among decision makers can take a variety of formats, ranging from unstructured and written notes to structured and numerical tables (Bernard, 1979). The most complex form of traffic is the situation in which decision makers simultaneously request information exchanges on different subjects from different members using complicated combinations of input/output formats. It would then be necessary to identify, classify and convert heterogeneous information styles into standard message formats, including the creation and maintenance of information related to group problem solving techniques, such as aggregation of preferences which requires some standardized inputs from individual results.

7.1.2 Limited versus Free Information Exchange

In some group decision situations, it is conceivable that all shared information is 'public' in that every member of the decision group has the right to access any information that is sent by one member of the group to another, whereas in some other decision situations, individual-to-individual or private message transfers are authorized (Deutsch and Krauss, 1962). Thus, the creation, (statistical) maintenance and storage of message routing activities remains crucial in enforcing group norms concerning the type of information sharing (e.g., consensually predefined by the group prior to the group decision-making process in Type 5 GDSS, or monitored by the mediator in Type 6 GDSS) (see section 4.1).

7.1.3 Evolving Pattern of Communication Requirements

The requirements for information sharing evolves through various phases of the group decision-making process. For example, Walton (1969) argues that a group problem-solving phase that emphasizes search and innovation requires more spontaneity, and therefore an open communications pattern; whereas, bargaining activities that induce a preference for deliberate control of information exchange would be facilitated by using individual-to-individual communication channels.

Furthermore, empirical studies have shown that, under certain circumstances, communication channels can escalate conflict (Krauss and Deutsch, 1966). While encouraging information exchange between group members is often recognized as an effective strategy to resolve individual differences, the strategy of eliminating communication channels has shown its effectiveness in preventing deterioration of relationships. While the decision to encourage or discourage communication between decision makers depends on a number of unpredictable situation-dependent factors, the GDSS communications component should be designed in such a way that it can accommodate various communications needs and changes during the group decision-making process. In other words, the pattern of communications protocols should vary according to the dynamics of the group decision-making process.

7.2 THE ROLES AND FUNCTIONS OF THE GDSS COMMUNICATIONS COMPONENT

One of the roles of providing communications support is to make it easier for each member of the group to electronically communicate without having to be concerned about detailed and complicated protocol procedures. This issue of user transparency is particularly crucial given the diversity, and consequently the complexity, of the communication requirements and facilities.

However, the effort to obtain ease of communication access is not unique to the design of group DSS. Rather, it has always been one of the most important objectives of computer networks design. Yet, one can identify at least three roles that are specific to a communications system in group problem solving. At different phases of the distributed decision process, the communications system can play the role of a coordinator, a detective, or an inventor.

DECISION PHASES	ROLE	FUNCTIONS
Situation Analysis/ Information Gathering/ Problem Definition	Coordinator	Provide maximum support for information exchange
Individual Decision Analyses	Detective	Enforce communication protocols
Group Decision Analyses	Inventor	Search for data compatibility- for group algorithms; sort data for diffusion

Figure 7.1. The Roles and Functions of the Communications Component

7.2.1 The Coordinator Role

Most problem solving activity begins with situation analysis and problem definition. Situation analysis is characterized by a (common) recognition that there exists an urgent and important problem to be solved. Once identified in the situation analysis, a problem is transformed in the problem definition phase in such a way that solutions can be generated, analyzed and selected. Eiseman (1977) and Kolb et al. (1984) emphasize that the success of information gathering and problem definition relies on the ability of the group to eliminate mistrust and threat that could cause group participants to withhold or distort information. Walton (1969) suggests that by installing a communication medium that follows some norms of fairness (e.g., equality of participation, preserving autonomy), information exchange can be more abundant and accurate. The communication component should thus coordinate various protocols to engender participants' confidence. Such protocols could include the ones that (i) assure each member can successively broadcast his/her ideas given a equal amount of time, or (ii) support teleconferencing to synchronize arguments.

7.2.2   The Detective Role

A decision maker's analysis could be distorted by (i) the individual's attempt to 'spy' on others' activities, or (ii) the influence of some members who try to take over an individual's responsibility. The communications component should then play the role of detective to prevent unwanted data exchange or temporarily disable all links, or prevent malicious modification of public data. Concurrently, decision makers tend to delay sending their individual results. The communications component should press its users to submit opinions before a given due date.

From a broader perspective, the detective role consists of enforcing communications protocols previously defined to drive the collective decision-making process.

7.2.3   The Inventor Role

The inventor role is an extension of the coordinator role. Given the complex nature of a collective decision problem and the diverse and unpredictable decision approaches adopted by the participants, the communications component should be able to detect incompatible information exchange, and, if possible, propose alternate formats. The inventor role implies (i) potential for tolerance to uncertainty in requests and needs for data transfers, and (ii) continued search for communications operations that facilitate information exchange (Davis and Smith, 1983). Thus protocols for distributed GDSS should be able to analyze, evaluate and determine the content of transmissible information, rather than simply perform a transport task.

To support these roles, the *functions* of the communications component are at least twofold. First, it monitors a broad spectrum of data transports during a group problem solving process. This transport function ranges from information exchange to information hiding, from selective and personalized routing to collective diffusion of data from public to private information. Second, the communications component coordinates various activities (i.e., initialization, operation during consensus search, negotiation and mediation) by making it transparent to the members of the decision group.

7.3 AN ARCHITECTURE OF THE COMMUNICATIONS COMPONENT

7.3.1   A Model of Reference

The architecture described below is based on the Open System Architecture OSA-RM (ISO, 1982). This model defines a framework for providing data communication links between systems. Specifically, five communication functions are specified: link establishment (generally in a switched network), transmission opening, data exchange, transmission terminating, and link releasing. The reference model proposes decomposition of the communication architecture into seven layers. The services offered by each layer are described in Figure 7.2. Also, the factors or parameters indicating the performance of the layers are included in the parentheses.

The reference to such a standard is justified by the fact that the use of an ISO Network Model would (i) minimize operating systems dependencies, (ii) simplify protocol interfaces, (iii) assure reliability, ease of maintenance and portability, and perhaps most important, (iv) facilitate the integration of communication protocols in GDSS.

1. Physical Layer	Arbitration of access to the transmission media (network topology)
2. Data Link Layer	Management of information transfers via an established data link (e.g., throughput, transit delay, error detection algorithm)
3. Network Layer	Network routing and switching (priority, delay, security, cost, grade of service)
4. Transport Layer	End-to-end transport of messages traversing any topological configuration (access control, throughput, transit, delay, residual errors, service availability, sequencing, flow control, accounting)
5. Session Layer	Maintenance of the state of the dialogue between nodes e.g., synchronization, delimiting of data (configuration of transport connections, dialogue type, type and quality of transport service used)
6. Presentation Layer	Management of formats including the format control phase, the data transfer phase, and the presentation termination phase (security, flexibility, correctness)
7. Application Layer	Support of service-oriented functions (reliability, flexibility, security, adaptability)

Figure 7.2. The Layers of the ISO Reference Model, Their Functions and Performance Factors

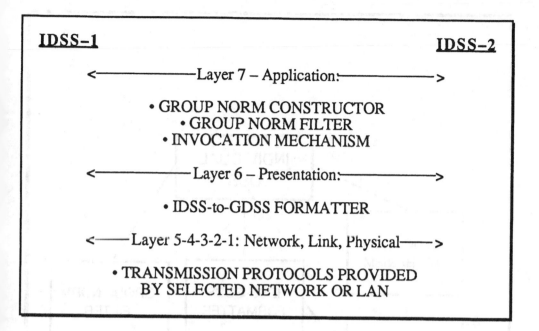

Figure 7.3. The GDSS Communications Component and the ISO Model

When applied to GDSS architecture – particularly, to type-5 and type-6 GDSS (defined in Chapter 2) in a distributed environment, the ISO modularity and hierarchy principles remain, but the internal logic of the first two layers will be adapted to the GDSS communication requirements. Starting from the Application level (i.e., layer 7), Figure 7.3 proposes an integration framework for the GDSS communications component into the ISO layering concept. Figure 7.4 illustrates the integration of the communications module in the individual DSS-group DSS link.

(1) The Application Layer in GDSS

In Layer 7, the purpose of the Group Norm Constructor is to provide a flexible and adjustable mechanism for monitoring communications transfers between individual DSS. This functional specialization is indispensable when a decision group has to define a framework for computer-based group decision making, and the GDSS does

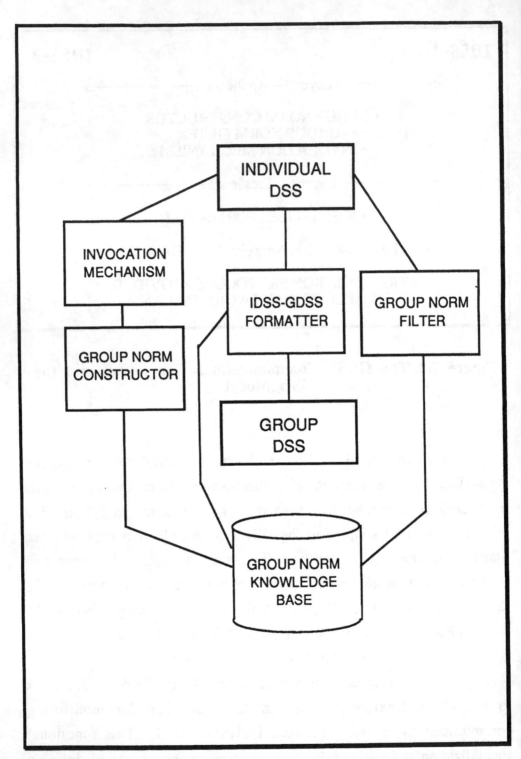

Figure 7.4. Four Modules of the Communications Component

not know in advance which type of communications should be invoked in a specific group decision situation.

The output that the Group Norm Constructor generates is a set of pattern-directed communications protocols that match the information exchange needs of the group members. This results in a consensually agreed upon set of rules governing communications contents (public and/or private), styles (predefined and/or free formatted information representation), channels (channeled and/or broadcast), frequency (maximum number of messages sent or requested), timing (deadlines for messages requests or answers; synchronized messages routing according to group decision-making stages). Figure 7.5 is an example of a group norm monitor.

This list of communications protocols is then sent to the Group Norm Filter. The function of this module is to enforce the defined protocols whenever a communication activity is triggered by the GDSS user. When a data transfer is requested, the Group Norm Filter will check whether or not the communication activity corresponds to the preset protocols. If the request is in accordance with the protocols, it is transferred to the next communications routine. Otherwise, the Group Norm Filter would notify the user of the violation, and, if requested, offer the group member the current communications protocols pattern. Figure 7.6 suggests some algorithms that could be used to implement a group norm filter.

DATA TRANSFERS:

- Point-to-point or private data sharing......................·____
- Maximum number of shared files ....·____
- Maximum size allowed for each file.......................·____
- File sharing allowed only at the following phases:
    - Problem definition ....·____
    - Individual Decision Analyses..........................·____
    - Group Decision Analyses ....·____

- Public data sharing..·____
- Maximum number of shared files ....·____
- Maximum size allowed for each file ....·____
- File sharing allowed only at the following phases:
    - Problem definition ....·____
    - Individual Decision Analyses..........................·____
    - Group Decision Analyses ....·____

INTERACTIVE CONVERSATION:

- On-line talk...·____
- Maximum number of talks ....·____
- Maximum time allowed for each talk.......................·____
- Talk allowed only at the following phases:
    - Problem definition ....·____
    - Individual Decision Analyses..........................·____
    - Group Decision Analyses ....·____

- Teleconferencing ....·____
- Maximum number of teleconferences.......................·____
- Maximum time allowed for each teleconf...................·____
- Talk allowed only at the following phases:
    - Problem definition ....·____
    - Individual Decision Analyses..........................·____
    - Group Decision Analyses ....·____

Figure 7.5. An Example of a Group Norm Constructor

ELECTRONIC MAIL:

- Point-to-point communication .... ____
- Maximum number of messages................. ____
- Maximum time allowed for each message..... ____
- Mail allowed only at the following phases:
    - Problem definition .... ____
    - Individual Decision Analyses............ ____
    - Group Decision Analyses................. ____

- Bulletin board..................................... ____
- Maximum number of messages................. ____
- Maximum time allowed for each message..... ____
- Mail allowed only at the following phases:
    - Problem definition .... ____
    - Individual Decision Analyses............ ____
    - Group Decision Analyses................. ____

GROUP DECISION TECHNIQUES:

- Automatic selection of aggregation of
    preferences techniques .... ____

- If NO,
    - Sums of the Ranks .... ____
    - Sums of Outranking Relations ...... ____
    - Additive Ranking .... ____
    - Multiplicative Ranking .... ____

- Automatic Computation of the Consensus
    Seeking Algorithm (NAI)............... ____
- Deadline for sending individual results...... ____
    - Date................................... ____/____/____
    - Time .... ____:____
- Broadcasting of individual results .... ____

Figure 7.5. An Example of a Group Norm Constructor
(continued)

```
IF        results-member-1 = "received"
          results-member-2 = "received"
THEN      select-group-algorithm
ELSE      check-deadline
ENDIF


IF        ind-result-deadline = "YES"
THEN      date              = set-date
          time              = set-time
          IF      current-date > date  AND  current-time > time
          THEN    select-group-algorithm
          ELSE    wait
          ENDIF
ELSE      wait
ENDIF


IF        auto-selection-of-AP = YES
THEN      select-appropriate-group-algorithm
ELSE      group-algorithm = set-group-algorithm
          compute-group-result
ENDIF


IF        MCDM-member-1 = AHP AND MCDM-member-2 = ELECTRE
          OR
          MCDM-member-1 = ELECTRE AND MCDM-member-2 = AHP
THEN      number-of-feasible-group-result = 1
          group-algorithm-1 = "Sums-of-Outranking-Relations"
          data-conversion(AHP-Sums-of-Outranking-Relations) = "necessary"
          compute-group-result
ELSE      number-of-feasible-group-results = 4
          group-algorithm-1 = "Additive"
          group-algorithm-2 = "Multiplicative"
          group-algorithm-3 = "Sums-of-the-ranks"
          group-algorithm-4 = "Sums-of-Outranking-Relations"
          data-conversion(AHP-Sums-of-Outranking-Relations) = "necessary"
          compute-group-result
ENDIF
```

Figure 7.6. An Example of Group Norm Filter Routines

Finally, the invocation mechanism enables the decision maker to request eventual modification of the communications protocols previously set via the Group Norm Constructor. The rationale of such a mechanism is to provide enough flexibility to deal with the inherently dynamic and nondeterministic communications nature of a group problem solving process. Moreover, a request for a protocol change from a group member can not be satisfied unless it is approved by the entire group. Triggered by a group member's request, the invocation mechanism checks when and how it can convene the decision makers to debate and vote on the motion.

(2) The Presentation Layer in GDSS

The particularity of the Presentation Layer in the GDSS communications architecture is the IDSS-to-GDSS Document Formatter. This formatter contains presentation protocols for any possible type of data exchange in a group decision situation. Examples of such protocols are those related to data structures that are shared between the IDSS Model Components and the GDSS Model component. For instance, in a voting procedure, data must be compressed before being reported to individual members.

SUMMARY

The design of a group decision support system necessitates careful analysis and design of communications capabilities. Communications support should go beyond establishment of reliable and efficient data transfers. This chapter proposed the creation of a communications component for GDSS. At different phases of the group decision process, the communications component can play three supporting roles: It can be a coordinator in that it provides support for various types of information exchange between group members; it can be a detective by enforcing group norms related to communication protocols; finally, it can be an inventor in that it helps search for data compatibility and sorts relevant information for diffusion.

This chapter also discussed architectural issues of the group DSS communications component. It suggested the use of the ISO network model. Specifically, the functional modules of the communications component (i.e., the group norm constructor, the group norm filter, the invocation mechanism and the IDSS-to-GDSS formatter) could be integrated into the last two layers of the ISO model.

Such an integration would not only minimize operating systems dependencies and simplify protocol interfaces, but facilitate the implementation of various group DSS architectures as well.

8. Co-oP SYSTEM ARCHITECTURE AND SOFTWARE COMPONENTS

This chapter describes Co-oP, a DSS for cooperative multiple criteria group decision support systems. The analysis and implementation of Co-oP provides some actual solutions to the conceptual considerations for designing multiple criteria group DSS outlined in chapters 4, 5, 6 and 7.

8.1 BRIEF REVIEW OF DESIGN ISSUES FOR BUILDING MC-GDSS

In chapter 4, six different types of group DSS architectures were addressed. The most complex architecture is characterized by multilateral relationships between members of a group via a network of individual DSS and group DSS. A strategy to design such a group DSS is to decompose the GDSS model component into individual and group model bases that support both content-oriented and process-oriented decision techniques (Chapter 5). The latter can be interfaced with the decision makers using a universal and unambiguous man-machine interaction style (Chapter 6). Furthermore, a GDSS should provide the users with a communications framework to help them shape the GDSS supporting capabilities with their decision environment. Such a framework can be implemented by setting communications parameters and group norms prior to the evaluation and decision phases of the group problem (Chapter 7).

8.2 OVERVIEW OF THE Co-oP SYSTEM ARCHITECTURE

8.2.1 Systems Overview

Co-oP is a network of microcomputer-based process-driven DSS for cooperative multiple criteria group decision making (Figure 8.1). Each participant of the group decision making process has his own individual DSS whose model base is based on multiple criteria decision methods (MCDM) and other personal decision support tools. The group DSS contains a set of aggregation of preferences techniques and consensus seeking algorithms that can be used in conjunction with individual MCDM.

The individual DSS are linked together by a microcomputer network system using a bus architecture and the Carrier Sense Multiple Access with Collision Detection (CMSA/CD) protocol. The particularity of the CMSA protocol resides in the fact that each workstation or node is required to 'listen' before transmitting. Also, if a collision occurs during transmission, the Collision Detection protocol forces both sending workstations or nodes back off random time intervals before trying again. The CMSA/CD protocol is known for its relatively good performance, simplicity of implementation, and inherent system reliability (National Bureau of Standards, 1982).

Co-oP is written in Turbo Pascal. It currently contains 16,000 thousands lines of Pascal codes using an overlay structure. When installed in a network, the compiled version of Co-oP is stored in the main server to allow group member to share the system resources and read/write file activities.

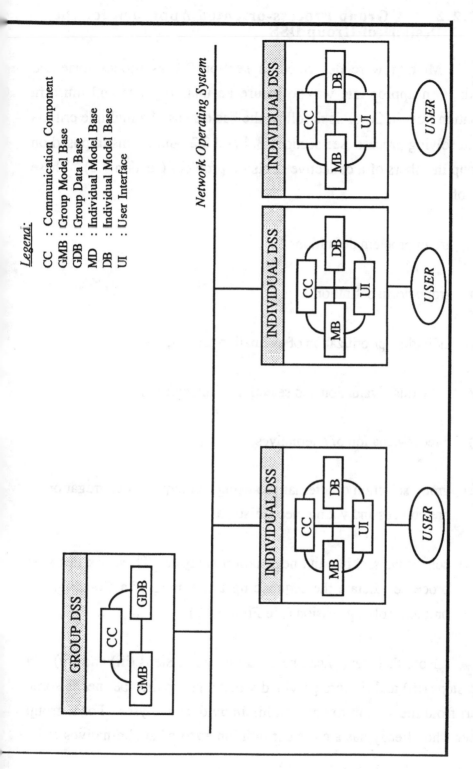

Figure 8.1. The Co-oP system linking Individual Workstations via a Computer Network

8.2.2 A Group Process-oriented Approach for the Design of Group DSS

MCDM were described in section 2.1 as process-oriented methods. An appropriate way to insure an unambiguous and uniform information flow in Co-oP is to follow the basic steps of a multiple criteria problem solving process (see sections 3.4 and 8.2) and norms imposed on the group members of a collective decision problem (section 7.2). These consist of:

(i)   group problem definition,

(ii)   group norm definition,

(iii)   individual prioritization of evaluation criteria,

(iv)   individual evaluation and selection of alternatives,

(v)   direct evaluation of alternatives,

(vi)   group selection of alternatives using techniques of aggregation of preferences and voting mechanism, and

(vii)   consensus seeking and negotiation analysis. These six decision processes dictate the sequencing and timing of a Co-oP group problem solving session (see Figure 8.2).

Note that step(v) can be used instead of steps (iii) and (iv). In effect, steps (iii) and (iv) are provided when a group member needs some support from the system to perform his individual analyses. For a group member who already has a clear-cut opinion as to what alternatives to be

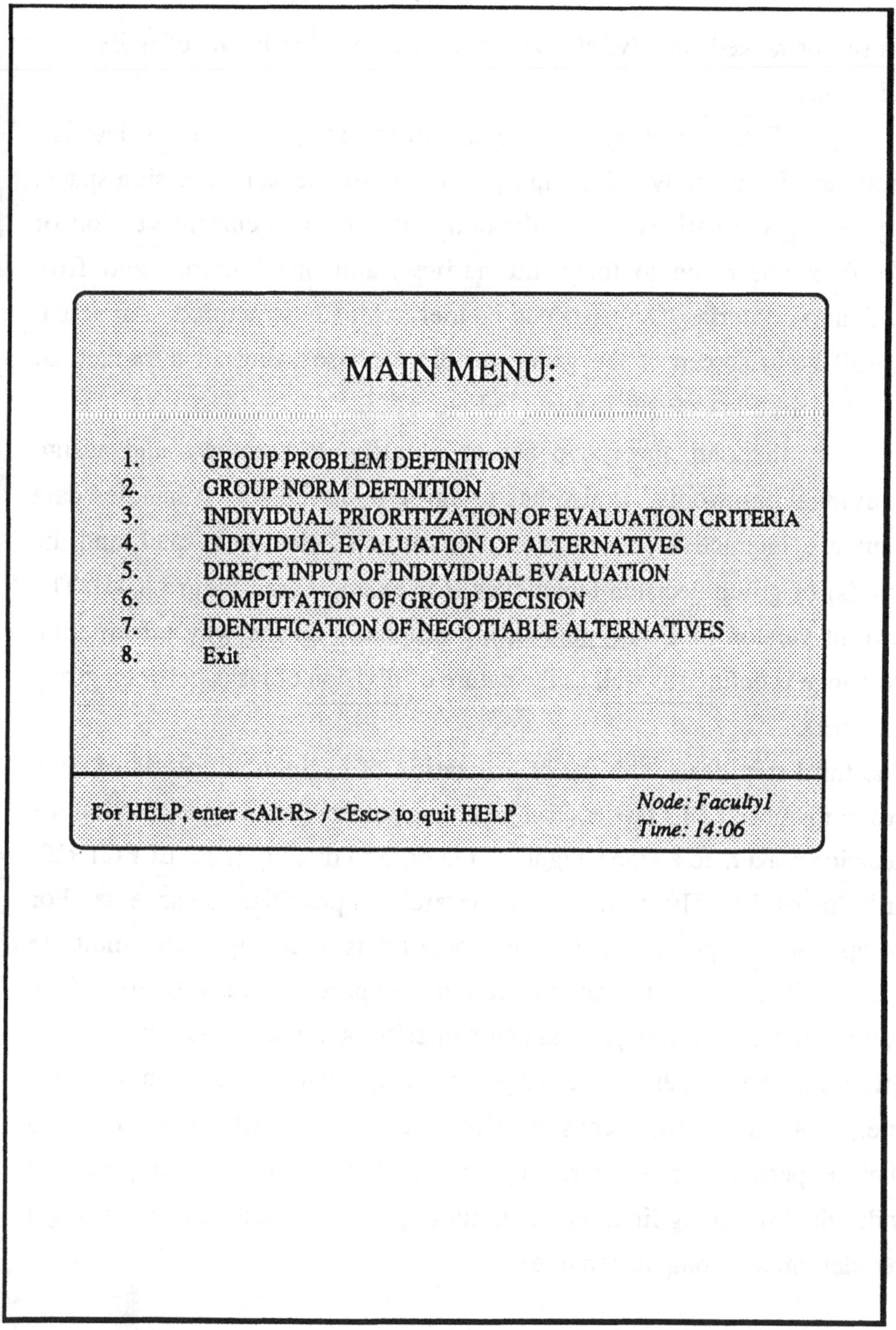

MAIN MENU:

1. GROUP PROBLEM DEFINITION
2. GROUP NORM DEFINITION
3. INDIVIDUAL PRIORITIZATION OF EVALUATION CRITERIA
4. INDIVIDUAL EVALUATION OF ALTERNATIVES
5. DIRECT INPUT OF INDIVIDUAL EVALUATION
6. COMPUTATION OF GROUP DECISION
7. IDENTIFICATION OF NEGOTIABLE ALTERNATIVES
8. Exit

For HELP, enter <Alt-R> / <Esc> to quit HELP

Node: Faculty1
Time: 14:06

Figure 8.2. The Process-driven Co-oP Main Menu

chosen or ranked, step (v) allows direct and un-aided inputs of individual solutions.

First, the group must collectively identify and define a decision problem. Specifically, all group members share the same decision space, e.g., same alternatives and evaluation criteria. The current version of Co-oP supports up to forty alternatives, and one hundred and fifty evaluation criteria. The latter can be hierarchically structured. An actual Co-oP input screen of the group problem phase using an hypothetical faculty selection example is given in Figure 8.3.

Second, the group has to identify its members and assign individual passwords. It also has to agree upon the way it handles data transfers, interactive conversation, utilization of electronic mail, and the type(s) of group decision techniques (for example, see Figure 8.4). The current version of Co-oP puts strong emphasis on the way information exchange is defined as well as the nature of division of tasks between group members.

The third step deals with the prioritization of evaluation criteria of each group member. This process can be either accomplished by requesting the decision makers to assign weights to the criteria directly (e.g., ELECTRE), or by using the AHP (Saaty, 1980) hierarchical prioritization scheme. For comparison purposes, this Co-oP process acts as a single user multiple criteria DSS with data communications support. Moreover, the Co-oP collective prioritization process can be performed in pooled mode (i.e., all group members enter 'collectively' a priority vector), in sequential mode (i.e., group members assigns priority to a subset of criteria according to their expertise), or in aggregation mode (i.e., each member performs individual weighing first; then individual priorities are aggregated using a pre-determined computation rule).

```
NAME OF GROUP PROBLEM : Faculty Selection

IDENTIFICATION  OF  ALTERNATIVES:
Type <q> to end definition of alternatives:

1. Jones
2. Smith
3. Newton
4. q

ENTER HIERARCHY OF EVALUATION CRITERIA
Type        <1> for first level,
            <2> for second level,
            <3> for third level, and
            <q> to end definition of evaluation criteria:

1.   Education
            1.1 Undergraduate
            1.2 Graduate

2.   Experience
            2.1 Teaching
                      2.1.1     Undergraduate
                      2.1.2     Graduate
            2.2 Research

3.   Area of specialization
```

Figure 8.3. An Input Screen of the Co-oP Group Problem Definition Process. (The underlined text is entered by the group leader or secretary).

Given a defined problem, the fourth Co-oP process allows the decision makers to individually evaluate alternatives using his preferred or familiar MCDM. Three individual MCDM are implemented in Co-oP (see section 8.5).

The next phase of the Co-oP process is the computation of group results using appropriate aggregation of preferences techniques.

Four techniques of aggregation of preferences have been implemented. They use the individual MCDM outputs to compute group results. Co-oP also allows weighing of users' decisional power (see section 5.2).

Finally, if unanimity is not obtained, a consensus seeking algorithm can be evoked in the sixth and last phase (see section 5.3). If impasse still prevails, decision makers can attempt to revise their problem representations by going back to any of the previous steps.

The decomposition of the group decision problem into processes also permits the user to momentarily interrupt his/her analysis at any Co-oP step. Similarly, he can log back into the decision support without having to start from the first process again.

During any phase of the group decision making process, the Group Communication System (GCS) interface will connect individual DSS to the group GCS upon request. Co-oP uses an electronic notepad (Borland, 1985) that runs concurrently with other Co-oP modules. This electronic notepad serves as a bulletin board that makes it possible for each decision maker to store, move, process and broadcast written communications or data among the group members in either formal or informal modes. An electronic mail system is also installed in the network to provide point-to-point communications.

8.2.3 A Content-oriented Approach for the Design of Co-oP Individual DSS

In each individual DSS, the Co-oP User Interface Component is characterized by a menu-driven window-based system that allows decision makers to access the Model Management System (MMS), and the MCDM-specific File Management System (FMS).

The MMS provides a technique-driven milieu for understanding, selecting, retrieving, and operating the decision models stored in the Content Oriented Model Bank (COMB) and the Multiple Criteria Decision Model Bank (MCDMB). The purpose of the COMB is to provide each individual decision maker with a large set of models to support the process of finding his personal solution to the group problem. These models can be classified into two broad functional classes: explicative models (e.g., linear programming, financial models), and time series models (e.g., regression models, smoothing techniques).

Three MCDM are stored in the MCDMB to support two types of decision; namely, the ELECTRE method (Roy, 1968) for selecting (i.e., to choose one and only one 'best' alternative among many), the multi-attribute utility model using an additive utility function and, the Analytic Hierarchy Process (AHP) (Saaty, 1980) for ranking (i.e., all alternatives are good but they are ranked according to the decision maker's needs).

The group model bank is linked to the individual MCDM via the Communications Component. The group MCDM computes or updates group results and stores them in the group file management system. The latter ensures that decision makers can freely use their individual DSS before committing to an opinion (see also section 4.3).

8.3 THE Co-oP MODEL COMPONENT

As described in section 8.2, the Co-oP model component consists of three modules: the MCDM model bank, the group model bank, and the consensus seeking module. This section justifies the implementation of the ELECTRE and AHP methods in Co-oP. It also explains the Co-oP group model bank and consensus seeking module.

8.3.1 The MCDM Model Bank

In Chapter 5, we argued for the design of a unified multiple criteria decision support system. Three advantages of such a system were discussed in section 5.4. These include (i) generalized support of a wide range of multiple criteria decision situations, (ii) reduction of costs of information searches, and (iii) flexible division of decision making tasks.

The main purpose of the Co-oP MCDM model bank is to provide the decision makers with a set of decision models that can solve the most common types of decision problems. The current version of Co-oP contains three models that (i) cover three basic decision situations, i.e., selection, ranking, sorting, (ii) are not excessively difficult to use for the decision makers, and (iii) could interact with techniques of aggregation of preferences (described in section 5.2). The Analytic Hierarchy Process (AHP) (Saaty, 1980), ELECTRE (Roy and Bertier, 1968).

ELECTRE and AHP have been selected for two reasons:

(1)   The two MCDM are conceptually robust, and practically easy to learn and use. They have proven their usefulness in aiding a number of ill-defined decision situations (for example, Pasquier et al., 1979; Heidel and Duckstein, 1983);

(2)   Neither ELECTRE nor AHP require full information on the decision maker's preferences and assessment of alternatives, and hence, give more autonomy and control to the decision maker (Crama and Hansen, 1983). This feature makes it easier to expand the algorithm to resolve group decision making.

Fifteen decision tools are included in the Supporting Model Bank. They include linear programming, transportation model, project scheduling, maximum flow, minimum spanning tree, shortest route, Bayesian probabilities, expected value analysis, decision tree analysis, Markow models, inventory model, linear regression, and queuing model. These models can be used concurrently in a multitasking environment. However, the current version does not support integrated data transfers between models.

This section briefly outlines basic concepts of the ELECTRE and AHP methods, and discusses their interactions within the Co-oP Model Bank. A complete mathematical formulation of these problems and solutions is discussed in (Roy, 1968; Bui and Jarke, 1984; and Saaty, 1980).

(1) The ELECTRE Method: Basic Concepts

ELECTRE is characterized by circumventing the problem of incomplete comparability of alternatives through its concept of outranking relations.

There are a number of reasons that make it difficult for a decision maker to exhaustively compare all known alternatives. First, the decision maker often cannot compare some alternatives, due to uncertainty associated with the measurements and evaluation. Second, the decision maker may be unwilling to compare two alternatives because they are incomparable; e.g., option a_i is better than option a_k by some criteria, whereas a_k is better than a_i by some other criteria. The notion of indifference in utility theory does not reflect this incomparability (Roy, 1976). Last but not least, the ill-structuredness and occasional inconsistency of the decision maker's preferences are serious obstacles to enforcing the complete comparability of alternatives (Saaty, 1980).

The concept of *outranking relations* seeks to compare decision alternatives only when the decision maker's preferences are well defined. In other words, a_i outranks a_k when the information obtained from the decision maker's preferences safely justifies the proposition that a_i is at least as good as a_k.

The outranking relation can be explained by two further concepts: the presence of *concordance* (i.e., for a sufficiently important subset of evaluation criteria, a_i is at least weakly preferred to a_k); and the absence of *discordance* (i.e., among the criteria for which a_k is preferred to

a_i, there is no significant discordant preference that would strongly oppose any form of preference of a_i over a_k).

These indexes are used in conjunction with concordance and discordance 'thresholds' chosen arbitrarily by the decision maker in the interval [0,1]. The concordance threshold, p, is more severe as it approaches 1; the discordance threshold, q, is more severe as it approaches 0. Then, the outranking relations can be summarized as follows:

IF	THEN
$c_{a_i a_k} \geq p$ and $d_{a_i a_k} \leq q$	a_i outranks a_k
a_i outranks a_k, and a_k outranks a_i	The alternatives are equivalent
Otherwise	The alternatives are incomparable

The decision maker can start with a less severe set of threshold values, and then sharpen them to reduce the number of outranking relations.

More formally, the ELECTRE algorithm is summarized as follows. Given a set of alternatives A, ($A = [a_i \mid i = 1,...,n]$), and a set of evaluation criteria E, ($E = [e_j \mid j = 1,...,m]$), the ELECTRE algorithm consists of the following steps:

1. *Assign weights to the criteria:* $W = [w_j \mid j = 1,...,m]$ with $w_j \geq 0$
    for all j and $w_j = 1$; and $\sum w_j = 1$

2. *Define an ordinal-to-cardinal grading table* that allows the decision maker to assign points to each grade: $G = [\ g_{hj} \mid h = 1,...,l;\ j = 1,...,m]$. This ordinal transformation allows the use of qualitative criteria, and gives flexibility in scaling all criteria. Often, the range of grades for important or heavily weighted criteria may be dilated to emphasize the discordance, (i.e., a small difference between ai and ak for an important criterion may be more crucial than a rather significant difference between the same two alternatives for a less important or slightly weighted criterion.);

3. *Evaluate the alternatives with respect to each criterion:* s_{ij} assigned to each a_i for each e_j, for $i = 1,...,n;\ j = 1,...,m$;

4. *Compute pairwise comparisons* by calculating concordance and discordance indexes: The concordance index $c_{a_i a_j}$ $(i, k = 1,...,n)$ is defined as follows:

$$c_{a_i a_j} = \sum_{\substack{j = 1 \mid s_{a_{ij}} \ge s_{a_{kj}}}}^{m} w_j$$

$c_{a_i a_k}$ is the sum of the weights of the criteria for with a_i is at least as good as a_k. In other words, the concordance index indicates to what extent an alternative is better than another. A perfect a_i will have $c_{a_i a_k} = 1$ for all k.

The discordance index $d_{a_i a_k}$ $(i, k = 1,...,n)$ is defined as follows:

$$d_{a_i a_k} = \frac{\text{Max}\left[\sum\limits_{\substack{j=1 \mid s_{a_{ij}} < s_{a_{kj}}}}^{m} (s_{a_{kj}} - s_{a_{ij}})\right]}{\text{Max}\left[\sum\limits_{h=1}^{1} (g_{hl} - g_{h1})\right]}$$

$d_{a_i a_k}$ is the maximum difference of the scores for which a_k is preferred to a_i. In other words, the discordance index indicates to what extent an alternative contains discordant elements that might make the alternative unsatisfactory. A totally unacceptable a_i will have a $d_{a_i a_k} = 1$.

5. *Identify non-dominated alternatives* by deriving outranking relations between alternatives. The outranking relation $o_{a_i a_k}$ (i, j = 1,...,n) is defined as follows:

$$o_{a_i a_k} = \left[\begin{array}{l} 1 \text{ if } c_{a_i a_k} \geq p \text{ and } d_{a_i a_k} \leq q \\ 0 \text{ otherwise} \end{array}\right.$$

where p and q are, respectively, concordance and discordance thresholds. They are arbitrarily chosen by the decision maker in [0,1]. The concordance threshold p is more severe as it approaches 1; the discordance threshold q is more severe as it approaches 0. The decision maker can start with a less severe set of threshold values, and then sharpen them to reduce the number of outranking relations.

6. Based on the outranking relations, *draw a directed graph* in order to identify a subset of A that contains non-dominated alternatives.

7. If the decision maker thinks that the non-dominated alternative(s) are consistent with his or her preferences, stop the computation.

8.   Otherwise, re-start the algorithm. If the decision maker wants:

—   to select new thresholds, go to step (5),
—   to re-consider the weighting scheme, go to (1),
—   to re-evaluate alternatives with respect to certain criteria, go
       to (3).

(2) The Analytic Hierarchy Process: Basic Concepts

The Analytic Hierarchy Process (AHP) is a MCDM method that attempts to support complex decision problems by successively decomposing and synthesizing various elements of a decision situation (Saaty, 1980). Like ELECTRE, AHP permits subjective and qualitative pairwise comparison of alternatives. Unlike ELECTRE whose concept is based on the notion of non-dominated alternatives, AHP has its foundation on the concept of *priority*. The latter can be defined as a 'level of strengths' of one alternative relative to another. Departing from a predefined priority scale, the decision maker is asked to build a positive reciprocal matrix of pairwise comparison. A vector of priority can be derived by computing the eigenvector of the reciprocal matrix. The property of the eigenvector resides in the fact that it is a consistency indicator. Consistency is obtained when pairwise comparisons are transitively and proportionally consistent.

Given the same mathematical definitions used in the previous section, the Analytical Hierarchy Process (AHP) algorithm can be very briefly described by the following steps:

1.   *Perform pairwise comparison of evaluation criteria* using a
       positive reciprocal matrix of dimension n, where n is the number
       of criteria or a subset of criteria to be prioritized. For n criteria,
       only $\frac{n\,(n-1)}{2}$ judgments have to be inputted into the matrix of

evaluation since the south west triangle of the matrix contains reciprocals of the coefficients of the north east triangle:

$$e_{ij} = \frac{1}{e_{ji}}$$

where e_{ij} is the decision maker's pairwise evaluation of criterion a_i against a_{jh}.

2. Based from the matrix of evaluation, *compute the priority vector* by computing the *eigenvector* of this matrix.

3. Since the construction of the evaluation matrix is based on subjective and possibly inexact judgment, inconsistency in performing pairwise evaluation may occur. Mathematically, consistency of a positive reciprocal matrix can be verified when its maximum or principal eigenvalue, say λ, is equal to its dimension n. As a guideline, the decision maker's judgment becomes more consistent as the value of λ gets closer to n. If inconsistency exists, decision makers should revise their judgmental evaluations.

4. When there are *more than one levels of hierarchies*, prioritization of primary criteria with respect to their impact on the overall objective should be first computed; then prioritize the subcriteria with respect to their criteria. Weigh the vectors of priority of subcriteria by multiplying the values of their coefficients.

5. For each evaluation criterion, *perform pairwise comparison of alternatives* using the same evaluation technique as used for the criteria. Add all vectors of priorities together to construct a matrix of evaluation of alternatives.

6. *Calculate the final vector of priorities* by multiplying the composite weighed vector of priorities by the matrix of evaluation of alternatives. The alternative that has the highest priority value should be ranked as the best candidate.

Additional algorithms are added to help measure the decision maker's consistency. These algorithms contrast the user's evaluation scores with (i) a randomly simulated score that represents the conceivably most irrational evaluation, and (ii) the eigenvalue that represents the most accurate consistency. When inconsistency occurs, heuristics is provided to enable the user examine the input values and to eventually revise initial judgments, and, if appropriate, modify them to improve overall consistency.

8.3.2   The Co-oP Group Model Bank

In section 5.2., eight techniques of aggregation of preferences were surveyed. The current Co-oP group model bank contains four of them. These include the additive function, the multiplicative function, the sums-of-the-ranks approach, and the sums-of-the-outranking-relations approach.

In conjunction with the techniques of aggregation of preferences, the weighed majority rule (see section 5.4) is also implemented to account for the distribution of decision power among decision makers. This rule allows the group members to differentiate their decisional power according to various degrees of expertise or organizational hierarchies.

Unless otherwise specified by the group norm (see section 8.4), the Co-oP group module automatically searches for all aggregation techniques that are compatible with the individual MCDM used. If AHP has been adopted by every group member for individual assessment of alternatives, all of the four implemented techniques will be computed, since the latter are compatible with the AHP in that they are based on cardinal preferences. However, the ELECTRE method can work only with the sums-of-the-outranking-relations and, to a certain degree, the sums-of-the-ranks-algorithms.

When both available MCDM are used concurrently during the fourth process, the Co-oP model manager automatically searches for group decision techniques that can accept inputs from both AHP and ELECTRE. When a single user alternately uses both available MCDM, the Co-oP model manager sequentially displays group results according to all possible combinations of individual methods.

8.3.3 The Consensus Seeking Module

To a degree, Co-oP supports concession making. In the ELECTRE context, it attempts to perform sensitivity analyses on the ELECTRE parameters. In the AHP context, it applies the expansion/contraction/intersection mechanism searching for possible negotiation clues.

(1) Consensus Seeking in ELECTRE

In concordance with the defined group norm, the Group Norm Monitor (see section 7.2) requests the Co-oP group module to identify the decision maker(s) who assigned extreme scores to the alternatives. In effect, the latter which suffer from low concordance and high discordance are responsible for the empty set of group non-dominated alternatives. The group module also indicates how much concession the group should obtain from 'extreme' decision makers, i.e., the difference between the individual extreme concordance (discordance) index and the group concordance (discordance) threshold.

Such a sensitivity analysis constitutes a point of departure for the group to start exchanging points of view and directions to reach agreement, and, if any, reducing tension. The group can then temporarily exit from ELECTRE, and use the electronic notepad to informally resolve these problems of control and of tension management (see section 4.3). If some concessions can be obtained, the participants can return to ELECTRE and modify evaluation scores accordingly. By switching back and forth between the individual DSS and the group DSS , the participants can perform 'sequential concessions'.

(2) Consensus Seeking in MAUT and AHP

When the MAUT and/or AHP methods are used by every group member, and techniques of aggregation of preferences fail to identify unanimity, the Negotiable Alternative Identifier (NAI) presented in section 5.3 can be used to explore the chance of reaching consensus. The NAI expansion/contraction/interaction mechanism can be automatically triggered by the group norm monitor (see section 7.2) or activated by the decision maker at the end of the group decision making process (i.e., Process 6).

8.3.4 Combined Use of MCDM and Techniques of Aggregation of Preferences

Section 5.5 argued for a unified MCDM framework. Such an attempt can be applied to the two MCDM implemented in Co-oP. Specifically, there are three possible levels of interaction between ELECTRE and AHP. First, ELECTRE, when used alone, assumes that the decision has a defined vector of criterion weights. AHP can help the ELECTRE user perform prioritization of evaluation criteria prior to the pairwise evaluation of alternatives. Second, when the size of a decision problem is large, the number of inputs required to perform the AHP method can be excessive. The Co-oP user can use ELECTRE as a sorting tool to reduce the problem size, and then utilize AHP (see section 5.5) or as a input interface for the MAUT model. Third, since the three methods refer to the same decision space (defined in the Co-oP first process), they can be concurrently used to verify the decision maker's consistency.

8.4 THE Co-oP COMMUNICATIONS MODULE

The communications component in group DSS should support at least the following functions: coordinate information exchange, enforce communication protocols, search for data compatibility for group algorithms, and sort data for diffusion (see Chapter 7). In the context of cooperative multiple criteria group problem solving, Co-oP provides these communications functions. Section 8.4.1 describes the functions and features of the Co-oP group norm constructor. Section 8.4.2 explains how the Co-oP group norm filter enforces communications set in 8.4.1.

8.4.1   The Group Norm Constructor

The Group norm constructor allows Co-oP users to define a framework for group decision making and communications exchange. At the beginning of the group MCDM process, a group member must be elected as a group leader. (In fact, selecting a group leader can actually be viewed as a multiple criteria decision problem). The latter is responsible for defining the group problem (Process 1) and the group norm (Process 2). The primary role of the leader is to help group member create a electronic group decision making setting and define agreeable norms. The latter is then stored in file created by the Co-oP group norm constructor.

Figure 8.4 illustrates the actual Co-oP group norm constructor using a hypothetical faculty selection problem. Identification of decision makers — i.e., name and password — is necessary to coordinate distributed decision activities. Since the group leader is the member who defines the norms, he only can enter his password during the group norm definition process. Other members of the group will be requested to provide their passwords from their individual workstations.

The group has to agree upon the way group decision techniques have to be computed. Co-oP needs to know what techniques of aggregation of preferences it must use to compute group results. It also needs to know which weighed majority rule it has to comply with.

Parameters governing the nature of information exchange must also be defined. Co-oP supports broadcasting of individual outputs. When this option is selected, individual outputs are public in that they are diffused to every group member's workstation. Otherwise, only group results are broadcast throughout the network.

The group members have to elect the possibility of allowing its members to modify individual analyses after diffusion of group analyses. The number of modifications must be given to the group norm constructor.

Finally, time limits can be set to press the group members to reach a decision (see section 4.3.2). Co-oP allows its users to set a time limit to submit individual results. Via its group norm filter, Co-oP will warn the decision makers that beyond the time limit late submission of individual results will be ignored.

To assist the group leader coordinate ideas and allow decision members communicate their opinion regarding the group problem solving process, a bulletin board system or electronic notepad can be concurrently used during the decision process. The latter is a form of format-free medium that allows group members to freely exchange ideas or portions of computer outputs.

```
ENTER THE NAME OF THE GROUP NORM              :      Norm1

1.  .IDENTIFICATION OF GROUP MEMBERS:
     1.1 Group Norm Builder Identification
         —    Your name                        : _ Chairman
         —    Your I.D.                         : ___ ******


     1.2 Enter number of decision makers
             (Maximum 15)                       :          2
         —    Enter name of decision maker
              No. 1                             : _ Faculty1
         —    Enter name of decision maker
              No. 2                             : _ Faculty2

2.  GROUP DECISION TECHNIQUES:
     2.1 Weighted majority rule:
         —    EQUAL Weights (Y/N)               :          Y

     2.2 Collective evaluation mode
             Choose one of the following modes:
                 <1> Each group member will
                     evaluate alternatives according
                     to ALL criteria
                 <2> Each group member will
                     evaluate only alternatives
                     according to his/her exclusive
                     area of expertise
             Enter a number                     :          1

     2.3 If more than one individual decision technique
             is used by a group member, which
             individual outcome to submit for group
             decision making?
                 <1> Last individual method used
                 <2> Method chosen by individual
                     group member
             Enter a number                     :          2
```

Figure 8.4.   The Co-oP Group Norm Definition Process for the faculty selection example (The underlined text indicates the user's input)

```
   2.4  Automatic selection of techniques of
             aggregation of preferences (Y/N) : _____ N
        —    R1 : SUM-OF-RANKS (Y/N)           : _____ Y
        —    R2 : SUM-OF-OUTRANKING-
                  RELATIONS (Y/N)              : _____ N
        —    R3 : ADDITIVE RANKING (Y/N)       : _____ Y
        —    R4 : MULTIPLICATIVE
                  RANKING (Y/N)                : _____ Y

   2.3  Automatic computation of NAI (Y/N)     : _____ Y

3.  INFORMATION EXCHANGE
   3.1  Broadcasting of individual outputs
             (Y/N)                             : _____ Y

   3.2  Permission to modify individual analyses
        AFTER group analyses (Y/N)             : _____ Y
        3.2.1     How MANY times (Maximum 10) : _____ 3

   3.3  Time limit to submit individual results:
        3.3.1     How MANY days (Max 30)       : _____ 3
        3.3.2     Hour (1 to 24)               : _____ 12
                  The deadline is 3-12-1986 at
                     12:00 pm (Y/N)            : _____ Y
        3.3.3     Broadcasting of group results to
                     group members who did NOT
                     submit  their analysis (Y/N): ____ Y
        3.3.4     Permission for LATE group
                     members to perform analysis
                     AFTER deadline (Y/N)      : _____ N
```

**Figure 8.4. The Co-oP Group Norm Definition Process for
the faculty selection example (Continued)
(The underlined text indicates the user's input)**

8.4.2   The Group Norm Filter

The function of the group norm filter is to enforce the norms defined in the group norm constructor. The Co-oP group norm filter resides in the group decision module. It performs three functions.

First, it grants access to group DSS facilities to an user only if his identification and password are correct. It also warns the users if the time is running out. Second, it keeps track of the number of data transfers from individual DSS to the group DSS. This allows Co-oP to deny unauthorized request to the group module. Finally, the group norm filter monitors computation of group decision techniques.

8.4.3   The Invocation Mechanism

As discussed earlier in section 7.3.1, group norms may have to be modified to deal with the inherently dynamic nature of a group decision problem. The invocation mechanism allows the users to change some previously defined norms that become unrealistic or unfeasible. Co-oP allows the group leader to modify a pre-defined group norm (Process 2). It also permits creation of alternate norms. Thus, many norms can be sequentially applied to a given decision problem, or a given norm can be used for different problem situations.

8.5 THE Co-oP INTERFACE COMPONENT

Section 6.2 and 6.3 discussed various issues related to the design of an user interface for group DSS. First, it particularly advocated a simple, unambiguous and standard man-machine interface to allow the participants concentrate on the core of the group problem. The Co-oP user interface was designed in such a way that it conforms as much as possible with these recommendations.

8.5.1   Screen Design

Despite the structured aspect of the multiple criteria group problem solving processes, it remains an eventual burden for the decision makers to memorize what he has done in the previous steps. Maintaining a high degree of coordination and cohesiveness of thoughts is particularly prevalent in complex decision problems (Mintzberg, 1971).

(1)   *Screen Format and Windowing:* During the problem definition and the group norm definition processes, data entry in *outline form* is adopted. Such an entry form would not only facilitate the thinking process of the managers, but also help decompose objectives into hierarchical levels (Saaty, 1980). Figure 8.2 exhibits examples of the outline forms used for defining the collective decision problem and the definition of group norms.

For the multiple criteria group decision processes (i.e., processes 3 through 7), Co-oP proposes a screen format that displays simultaneously four different windows (Figure 8.5). Whenever possible, Co-oP uses the same screen format throughout its usage. The purpose of such a design is to provide the user with a synoptic and familiar snapshot of the current state of the problem, throughout the entire decision-making process.

The *Step window* located at the bottom screen keeps the decision maker up to date on the current decision making status. It consists of a two-line status text indicating alternatively the current step in the hierarchy of group problem processes, and any required prompts or diagnostic messages related to the DSS-user interaction.

The *Dialogue window* provides a conversational medium between the decision maker and the DSS. It enables the Question/Answer mode of interaction to be accompanied by verbal and color/graphic explanation of various processing sequences and intermediate results.

To support the decision maker's orientation during the group decision-making process, the *Working window* at the upper left corner of the screen reminds the user of vital information from past dialogue or inputs. Also, it displays the results obtained by other participants if requested (see section 8.4.2).

The *Solution window* is located at the upper right of the screen. It displays intermediate and final results including statistical indexes, and highlights optimal values. Tabular outputs and bar graphs are combined to provide alternate ways to represent outputs.

In addition to the above mentioned windows, an electronic notepad window and the electronic mail box can be popped-up at any time to make use of person-oriented and unstructured communications.

(2) *Color and Graphics:* Throughout the entire Co-oP process, the windows can be recognized by their colors. Due to the limited size of windows, arrow keys are used to allow the user scroll through the data (e.g., number of decision makers, number of decision alternatives, and number of evaluation criteria).

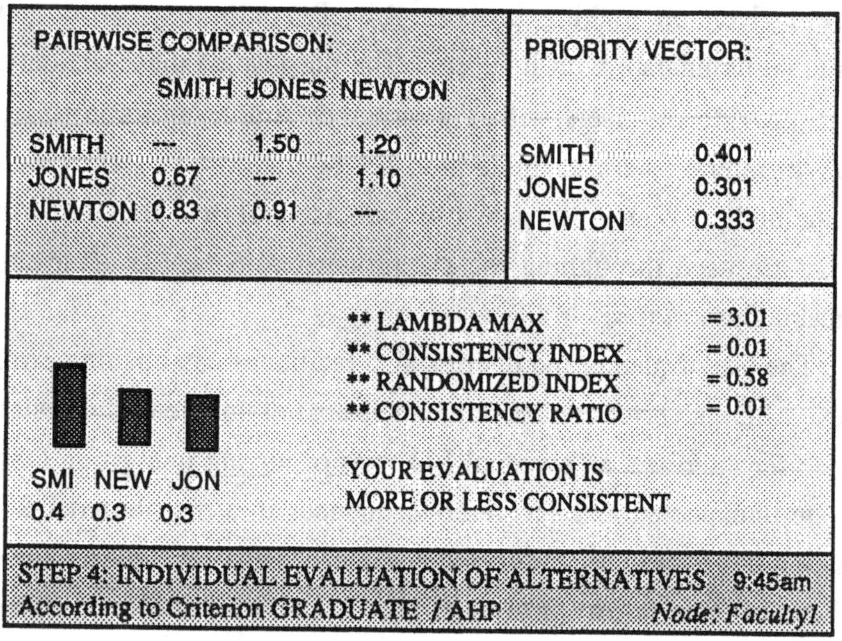

Figure 8.5. An Actual Co-oP Screen showing simultaneously
the Working, Solution, Dialogue and Step Windows

Whenever relevant, bargraphs and charts are displayed to provide the user with a visual presentation of the problem output.

8.5.2   Dialogue Style

In addition to the window structure that governs the entire Co-oP group decision making process, Co-oP combines menus and questions to communicate with its users. The purpose of these dialogue styles is to provide the users with a structured, simple and controlled framework to interact with an integrated set of multiple criteria group decision methods. Whenever possible, concise queries and uniform terminology are used throughout the six processes of the Co-oP group decision making process.

The use of menus and queries also facilitates establishing error procedures. Although error control procedures are not unique to the design of multiple user interface, an eventual I/O error occurring in a group DSS can generate unexpected and severe consequences in a distributed DSS. Input control routines have been implemented at each entry level to minimize the likelihood of input errors, or to maximize the possibility of recovering from errors when the latter occur.

To make it as insensitive as possible to errors made by the users, Co-oP provides two types of error control procedures. The first type of procedure detects syntax errors. For instance, entering a negative number of decision makers or typing an invalid filename would be gracefully rejected by the Co-oP dialogue manager. The second type of control routines attempts to prevent decision makers from violating basic assumptions or rules of the decision methods. For instance, the dialogue manager will refuse a concordance threshold higher than 100 percent when ELECTRE is used.

Co-oP also generates short explanation messages in the Step window to maintain the occasional user's confidence in the system, or at least make the multiple criteria group decision making less unnatural to the users.

8.6 THE Co-oP DATA FILE COMPONENT

The current version of Co-oP is a process-centered group DSS, as opposed to a data-centered DSS (for instance, see Jarke et al., 1985). As a consequence, the structure of the Co-oP data component is minimal. Its objective is to (i) insure smooth and fast data transport from one MCDM step to the other, and (ii) facilitate data exchange between decision makers. Figures 8.6 describes the most important portion of the Co-oP Data Flow Diagram.

Data files are grouped according to each process. These include (i) a file containing the problem definition (Process 1), (ii) a norm file for each group norm, (iii) a solution file for each group members, and (iii) a group results file for each decision problem.

To minimize the time needed for data transfers between individual workstations, group data files are physically centralized and stored in the server of the Local Area Network. However, they are functionally distributed in that they can be accessed only by authorized group members. However, individual working files are stored in local workstations.

SUMMARY

This chapter discussed the implementation of Co-oP, a DSS for cooperative multiple criteria group decision making. The realization of Co-oP has provided some solutions to the design requirements advanced in earlier chapters. In particular, Co-oP is a process-driven group DSS. Governed by a group DSS module and a communications component,

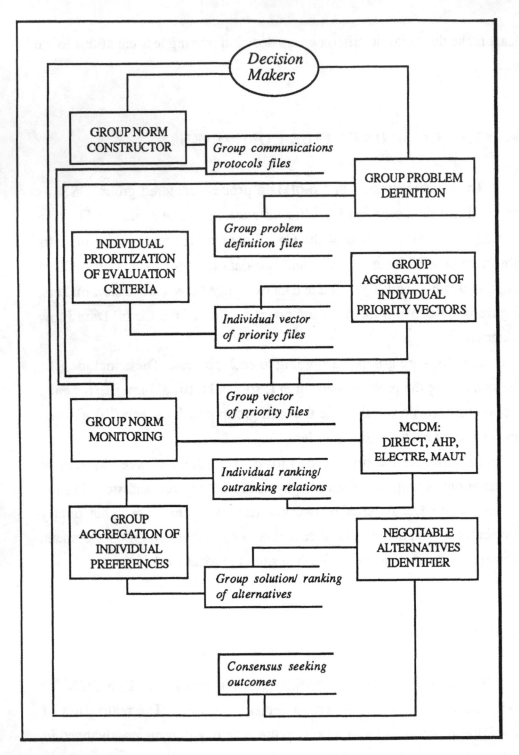

Figure 8.6. A Data Flow Diagram for the Co-oP MCDM Processes

Co-oP can support aggregation of preferences and, to a degree, consensus analyses.

The emphasis on the group processes has made it possible to build a generalized distributed DSS. First, the Co-oP decision making process can be applied to almost any multiple-criteria, multiple-person decision problem. Second, given the non-deterministic nature of group decision situations, Co-oP allows definition of multiple group norms. Such a feature would allow Co-oP to be shaped to specific group decision needs. Moreover, Co-oP permits the generation of multiple group norms to deal with the inherently dynamic nature of the group decision making process.

In addition, the adoption of a loosely-coupled group DSS architecture seems to increase the flexibility of the group decision support. By choosing various communications parameters and/or selecting various subsets of the Co-oP decision processes, Co-oP can take various forms of group decision architectures.

Finally, the modular architecture of Co-oP would make it possible to expand the support capabilities of the DSS. First, additional individual MCDM can be implemented in the Co-oP model base. This would gradually transform the current version of Co-oP into a generalized multiple criteria decision support system. Second, more restrictive norms could be gradually integrated to allow Co-oP to support some forms of non-cooperative or competitive decision making.

9. EVALUATION ISSUES FOR GDSS

In previous chapters, we have focused on issues related to the general design and specification of various functional modules of group decision support systems. The description of Co-oP in chapter 9 illustrates this analysis. However, the evaluation process should be considered in the GDSS building process. System builders must realize that GDSS may not be a panacea for all group problems and must identify those problems for which a specific GDSS is appropriate before GDSS can gain acceptance by group users.

Evaluation has been one of the most difficult tasks of DSS development because most DSS are (i) evolutionary in nature, (ii) incomplete by the time evaluation is needed, and (iii) there does not exist a unique way to measure DSS performance. Keen and Morton (1978) survey a number of methodologies that could be used to measure change in the decision making process induced by DSS usage. These include evaluation schemes based on decision outputs, changes in the decision process, changes in managers' concepts of the decision situation, procedural changes, cost-benefit analysis, service measures, value analysis and even anecdotal evidence. As an emerging technology, GDSS deals with a significantly more complex environment than typical individual DSS. applications (Huber, 1984; Gallupe, 1986). The primary goal of GDSS is not simply to automate existing facets of group processes but rather to enhance, or 'value add' to, the group decision making process. This requires a more extensive model of GDSS effectiveness than has currently been proposed, a model that considers the broader issues of group dynamics, communication effectiveness, corporate culture, and unique problem types.

This chapter overviews current propositions to evaluate GDSS and propose a contingency model of effective GDSS use as a function of one of the most critical organizational parameters — problem types. The purpose of the model it to help identify prime organizational problem solving opportunities for GDSS use (Suchan, Bui and Dolk, 1987).

9.1 REVIEW OF GDSS FROM AN EVALUATION PERSPECTIVE

Because GDSS research is in its infancy, there exists only a small body of literature from which to draw. Most treatments of GDSS concentrate on its design rather than on identifying the appropriate organizational settings for its use.

9.2.1 GDSS Based on IDSS Criteria

Although there is currently nothing in the literature which attempts to evaluate GDSS using IDSS criteria, Keen (1981) has suggested value analysis as an approach to justifying DSS. Value analysis is a slight variation of prototyping which requires that a prototype be built and then a benefit threshold identified to determine the feasibility of building a full version of the prototype. The premise behind value analysis is that a quick and inexpensive initial version of a DSS can be built which then forms the basis for determining ultimate benefits.

Value analysis, if applied to GDSS, would require DSS prototyping capabilities that could be transferred to a group setting. It is doubtful, however, that a GDSS prototype can be built as easily as an IDSS prototype given the more complex decision making environment it must support (see Chapter 7 for a description of the elaborate communications requirements for GDSS). This places added emphasis on the importance of identifying those problem-solving situations, a priori, which are most likely to complement GDSS use.

9.2.2   GDSS Based on Communications

Another proposed framework to evaluate GDSS is to examine how GDSS can be effective as a novel channel of communication between decision members. Jarke (1986) identifies four group communication situations: (i) spatial distance, (ii) temporal distance, (iii) centralization of control, and (iv) degree of cooperation. Evaluating GDSS consists thus of measuring the effect of GDSS in supporting these communication settings.

Focusing on these settings makes a great deal of sense since group problem solving is fundamentally an issue of intense interactions between different participants; consequently, the various settings that computer networks offer create significantly different communication channel problems. However, assessing the appropriate use of these channels to maximize GDSS use in collective problem solving is difficult to say the least. Research found by social psychologists on human communications can hardly be applied to this communication channel problem (Short et al., 1976).

9.2.3   GDSS Based on Frequency-of-Use and Group Activity

Huber (1984) suggests that a GDSS must attain a minimum threshold of frequency-of-use in order to gain acceptance within an organization. This threshold, in turn, requires GDSS capabilities which support a critical mass of group tasks (Figure 9.1). Consequently, GDSS design strategy should focus on general group activities rather than trying to identify and support all possible group tasks. These group activities are identified as information sharing, use, and analysis.

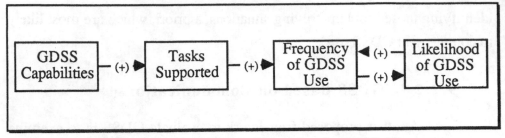

Figure 9.1. Huber's Model of GDSS Use

Huber contends that the greater the number of group tasks a GDSS supports, the higher its frequency-of-use will be. This argument is somewhat misleading since sophisticated system capabilities may also make GDSS more difficult to use. Again, one can argue that frequency-of-use is more likely to result from carefully identifying those group problems in which GDSS can 'value add' rather than building a GDSS generator with general capabilities.

9.2.4   GDSS Based on Task Difficulty

Gallupe (1986) has conducted preliminary experiments which center on group task difficulty as the major independent variable in the GDSS setting. Dependent variables measured were decision quality, the time required to make a decision, and group confidence in the decision made. Both Huber and Gallupe recognize the importance of group task in determining the effectiveness of GDSS. With this one exception, however, there seems to be little, if any, discussion about which organizational variables play an important role in the acceptance and use of GDSS. Although group task undoubtedly needs to be considered, group environments present a wide range of other issues in the areas of group dynamics, communication effectiveness, corporate culture, and problem solving.

9.3 A CONTINGENCY MODEL FOR ASSESSING EFFECTIVE USE

9.3.1   GDSS and Problem Types

To determine when a GDSS could 'value add' to a group's problem solving capabilities, we need to examine carefully the types of problems a GDSS could help solve. Unfortunately, GDSS researchers have sidestepped the knotty problem of devising a problem classification system that could help managers and high-level executives decide whether GDSS would improve or impede their groups' problem-solving processes. And it is precisely this lack of a problem classification system that has caused GDSS researchers to overgeneralize about the corporate benefits of GDSS use in group problem-solving situations.

Researchers in organizational behavior, particularly those interested in leadership and problem solving, have indirectly suggested a problem classification system that can be used to create a model which can help managers perform a relatively simple risk/benefit analysis of GDSS use in various broadly defined group problem-solving situations.

Likert (1967), Szilagyi and Wallace (1980), and Vroom and Yetton (1973), among others, have found that managers generally fall into two categories: task- and relationship-oriented. Task-oriented managers focus on finding the specific algorithm or procedure to solve a problem (often technical by nature) and on either implementing the solution themselves or delegating the implementation to their subordinates. On the other hand, relationship-oriented managers stress the maintenance and strengthening of the group that would be affected by the decision outcome.

Not surprisingly, task-oriented managers are most successful when solving problems of a particular type — those that deal with technical procedures or operations such as a complex inventory control problems or an analysis of the benefits of one accounting system over another. In essence, their minds reflects a mechanistic view; the organization is basically a machine that can be made to run well by rational, model decision making and bureaucratization (also see Chapter 12).

In contrast, the relationship-oriented managers excel at problem solving that affects people, their morale, and their motivation. These managers skillfully maneuver the interpersonal complexity required to actually implement (rather than merely plan) the structurization of a department. Their problem-solving strategies are not exclusively linear or model based but reflect recursive, elliptical thinking where intuition, hunches, and 'vision' become a primary mode of problem solving.

Obviously this classification scheme oversimplifies the complexities of managers and of problem-solving situations they face in the rough corporate environment. Nevertheless, it provides GDSS researchers a broad-based but useful classification scheme for problem types.

9.3.2 Task-oriented Problem and Relationship-oriented Problem

Hitherto, the terms 'task' and 'relationship' are used to define these two general problem types. Their definitions are extended below.

Task-oriented problems require precise, linear thinking. These problems are usually well-defined, technical and highly structured. They often require the analysis of significant amounts of data. Portfolio management decisions, financial analysis problems, operational planning decisions — the coordination of departmental and divisional budgets for example — and marketing channel decisions can be classified as task-oriented problems. Solutions to task-oriented problems generally have a minimal impact on people in the organization.

Relationship-oriented problems are relatively unstructured problems. They call for empathetic thinking rather than merely analytical thinking. Managers or decision makers must often use 'vision', 'insight', 'intuition', 'gut response', and other forms of problem-solving strategies not derived from traditional, relatively formal analytic processes. Acquisitions and mergers, department and divisional reorganizations, and even long-range forecasting are examples of this type of problem. Solutions to these problems have an impact on the formal and informal values and norms of behavior (in the broadest sense) held by the corporate staff and employees as well as the 'cultural' or internal environmental makeup of the department, division, or corporation.

To account for the fact that problems are neither exclusively task nor relationship oriented, these categories can be viewed as a continuum that can be depicted in the following manner:

High and low refer to the degree that a problem is either task- or relationship-oriented. Also, both qualifiers are related to problem complexity — generally the higher the task or relationship orientation of the problem the more complex it is.

9.3.3   Explication of the Contingency Model

The following model focuses on the relative effectiveness of GDSS use in relation to general problem types (see Figure 9.2).

156

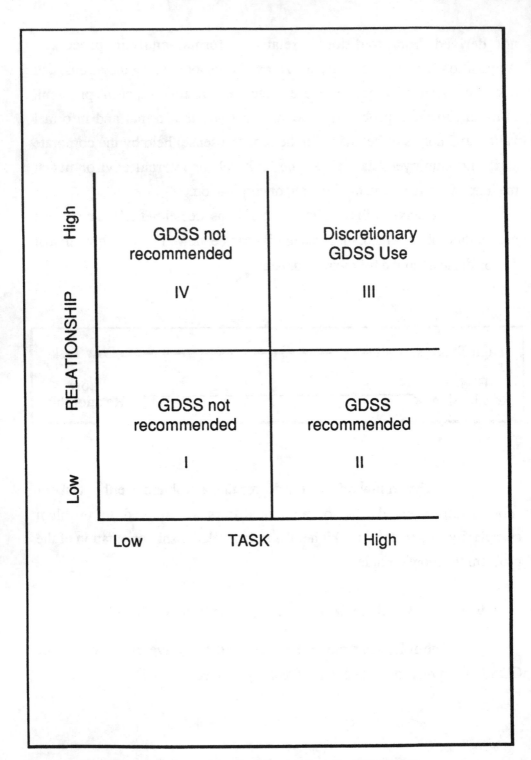

**Figure 9.2. A Contingency Model of GDSS Use
(Suchan, Bui and Dolk, 1987)**

HIGH RELATIONSHIP/LOW TASK:

GDSS use for problems of this type is not recommended.

Relationship-oriented problems neither lend themselves to the sophisticated model building that GDSS promotes nor translate into cause and effect relationships that can be easily analyzed. The variables at work in these problem types involve extremely complex interpersonal and intrapersonal relationships, psychological factors such as power, trust, ego, motivation, and morale, and a range of unconscious variables that affect not only the individual but also the group and even the corporation as a whole. Because these variables are difficult to quantify or even assign accurate weights to, the scientific, model-oriented method of decision making that GDSS promotes would be of limited use in solving these problem types.

Also, it is conceivable that using GDSS to solve a high relationship/low task problem could actually impede a group's ability to generate satisfactory solutions because GDSS may be the wrong communication channel to use. Every channel, whether it is writing, speaking, or teleconferencing, affects not only the type of information that passes through it but also how the receiver of that information will use it to make decisions. The highly structured method of information processing in GDSS may direct the group's problem-solving processes along narrowly prescribed lines that may prevent the group from engaging in a wide-ranging, elliptical discussion that could generate valuable solutions to high relationship/low task problems.

Finally, when solving complex relationship-oriented problems, group members often have hidden agendas — decision solutions generated for political reasons, for example — that cause them to avoid sharing accurate information, opinions, and perceptions. In the public sector, where keeping the bureaucracy running smoothly takes precedence over making a profit (which is obviously the bottom-line in the private sector), every decision, particularly high relationship ones, is fundamentally a political decision because its outcome affects power and territory. Consequently, political considerations are a hidden agenda in virtually every problem-solving situation. In the private sector, hidden agendas often operate in departments or organizations undergoing stress or in vertically structured organizations where hierarchical power significantly affects the decision-making process. Since the basis of GDSS success is a cooperative decision-making environment where trust and the sharing of information are given, it is plausible that GDSS would not be successful in helping to solve high relationship problems where powerful, hidden agendas are operating among group members.

HIGH TASK/HIGH RELATIONSHIP:

GDSS is recommended to solve this type of problem. However, we urge that GDSS be integrated with other methods of problem solving.

High task/high relationship problems, such as reorganizing a company division, introducing a comprehensive word and data management system to a company, or launching a new product line, call for systematic linear thinking as well as creative, non-structured, elliptical thinking. For example, when determining if a company should develop a new product line, decision makers must crunch numbers but not people. The decision group must assess huge amounts of demographic and consumer preference data provided by the Marketing Research department. GDSS could easily support manipulation of this data in different combinations so that a range of decision alternatives could be explored quickly and efficiently. Through the analysis of the various decision alternatives, consensus could be more easily reached because group members have had opportunity to discuss and debate multi-perspective solutions and recommendations.

However, numbers do not tell the whole story when decision makers determine whether to launch a new product or to tackle other kinds of high task/high relationship problems. Obviously the significant impact that the decision will have on the people in the organization must be factored into the decision.

As discussed earlier, the analysis required to make an effective relationship-oriented decision runs counter to the quantitative model building mode of thinking that GDSS so well supports. Since high relationship problems are often fraught with hidden agendas, power plays and a range of non-rational, unconscious responses, the linear model of decision making that GDSS supports should be deemphasized here. At this stage in the decision process decision makers need to use a more adaptive, interpretive method of decision making that places emphasis on intuition, 'street smarts' and 'vision' and that recognizes the impact that various decision alternatives will have on the department's, division's, and even the organization's culture.

LOW TASK/LOW RELATIONSHIP:

GDSS is not recommended to solve this problem type.

The reasons are fairly obvious. Low task/low relationship problems are not complex enough to justify GDSS use or even a group decision. It would be expensive from both a system and manpower standpoint to solve problems that could be handle a competent individual. Indeed, low task/low relationship problems are best handled by individual decision makers. However, if task complexity reaches a mid-range of difficulty, than an IDSS could be used to help generate decision alternatives.

HIGH TASK/LOW RELATIONSHIP:

GDSS is highly recommended to support high task/low relationship problems.

High task problems such as operational planning or department and divisional budgeting need a analytical, model, multiple perspective approach toward problem solving. Mintzberg (1973) has shown that managers are neither systematic planners nor careful conceptualizers when forced to solve complex problems requiring strategic planning. These activities in many cases are no more than rigid exercises where the participants are more concerned with controllership than generating creative solutions (Quinn, 1980).

The number of complex, interdependent, data-based variables at play in a high task/low relationship problem requires a problem-solving system to have the same amount of variety and complexity in its control mechanisms as the problem itself contains. GDSS seems to have the requisite variety of problem solving features to match the complexity of the problems it is trying to help solve. Furthermore, as discussed in previous chapters, with the wide range of operations it can perform, GDSS supports the multiple perspective approach toward problem solving that a complex, high task problem demands. The more complex perspectives a GDSS can undertake, the greater the likelihood that decision makers will address the complexity of the problem and its solving and avert the tendency of a cadre of decision makers to produce and analyze only that data that conform to their viewpoint.

As with any model which tries to capture the complexity of problem-solving, the contingency model presented here treats only some of the several factors that managers must consider before determining whether GDSS would value add to a group's problem-solving ability. Despite these limitations, the model does provide an important and comprehensive guideline for managers. Furthermore, the model opens more avenues for

GDSS research — particularly in the empirical vein — that can eventually help corporations make intelligent decisions about the appropriateness of GDSS use.

SUMMARY

This chapter addressed the critical aspect of evaluation in the GDSS development process. At the risk of dating ourselves, we sought to identify organizational opportunities for GDSS use. Based on a classification scheme of organizational problem types and the current technology, a four-cell contingency model was proposed. As the model implies, GDSS should be used with discretion by organizations because the system is presumably useful to help solve only high tasks/low relationship and, to a lesser extent, high task/high relationship problems. As detailed in Chapter 12, GDSS's ability to generate multi-perspective decision alternatives, to digest and model vast amounts of data, and to help group members reach consensus would make it an ideal tool for facilitating group processes to solve these two problem types. However, as the model suggests, GDSS could be counterproductive to help solve both high relationship/low task and low task/low relationship problems. For the former problem type, a less structured, more creative and intuitive form of decision making is called for, and for the latter type an individual decision maker with perhaps the help of an IDSS should be used.

Obviously, our model can be expanded to account for a variety of other organizational factors that influence effective problem solving and thus the wise use of GDSS as a problem-solving tool. In fact, the four cells in our model structure could be broken down to finer structures. More than just problem types should be examined to realistically assess the complex organizational environment that determines whether GDSS can contribute to solving complex management problems (see also Chapter 12).

10. FACE-TO-FACE GDSS VERSUS DISTRIBUTED GDSS: SOME EMPIRICAL EVIDENCE

This chapter relates the results of an experimental study on the effectiveness and efficiency of Co-oP in two specific implementations of GDSS in group decision settings: distributed GDSS and non-distributed or face-to-face (F-T-F) settings (Bui et al., 1987). Section 10.1 raises some general issues in conducting experimental design and alternate modes for research settings. Section 10.2 describes the laboratory experiment focusing on contrasting the impact of GDSS use in distributed and F-T-F meetings. Section 10.3 reports the experimental results.

10.1 PROBLEMS IN CONDUCTING EMPIRICAL RESEARCH IN GDSS

In chapter 9, we presented an evaluation model which we believe that it can be served as a viable framework for experimental studies. Regardless of the framework used to predict the potential usefulness of GDSS, it seems however natural to first compare computer-mediated tools and F-T-F interactions as two different modes of collective problem solving. Nevertheless, such an experimental approach is often tempered by the difficulties of isolating control variables caused by inhibiting factors present in the interactive group decision-making processes (Gallupe, 1986; De Sanctis and Gallupe, 1986). For example, Van De Ven and Delbecq (1974) enumerate a number of factors or variables that can affect the effectiveness and efficiency of group decision making:

- a 'focus effect' wherein interacting groups 'fall into a rut' and pursue a single train of thought for long periods;

- the 'self-weighing' effect, wherein an individual will participate in the group to the extent that he feels equally competent with others;

- pressures for conformity and implied threat of sanctions from the leader or knowledgeable groups;

- a tendency to reach speedy decisions before all problem dimensions have been considered.

Until proven otherwise by elaborate experimental studies, it seems that the above factors might exist as well in computer-mediated meetings, making it difficult for researchers to conduct empirical research differentiating GDSS and non-GDSS use.

Another avenue, probably less difficult but however not less consequential, is to focus on the use of networked computers to support distributed decision making. With the advent of communications technology and a GDSS communications architecture discussed in chapter 7, it is now possible for the decision makers who are dispersed in time and space to participate in a group decision making process. Referring to the attempt to compare computer-mediated and face-to-face interactions, some of the more frequently expressed comments are that (i) mediation diminishes the social impact, (ii) managers are action-oriented and prefer face-to-face communications, and (iii) use of computer-mediated systems may result in the lessening of interpersonal relationships and a loss of the richness of interaction. However, it is important to note that these findings were derived from experimental studies that used audio/video teleconferencing as computer-mediated systems. From a decision support system viewpoint, teleconferencing can be viewed only as a novel way of providing communicating support as opposed to supporting group decision to the group problem-solving process (see also section 3.3.2). As such, to better understand the impact of GDSS use, it is important that decision support capabilities, combined with various communications modes, be integrated to what has been called computer-mediated systems.

For this purpose, four scenario settings have been designed (Figure 10.1). The first setting depicts the situation in which decision makers try to solve a strategic problem in a F-T-F meeting. The second setting involves a distributed but noncomputer-assisted decision environment. Each decision maker solves the problem individually in his/her office and sends the solution to a higher-level manager for final decision. The third setting simulates a decision context in which managers meet in one room and share a GDSS. The fourth and last setting constitutes a distributed decision-making environment. Here the decision makers are located in different locations with access to the GDSS via a computer network.

These four configurations offers a number of experimental settings that GDSS research can take place in. Furthermore, we contend that if both GDSS in the third and fourth scenarios share the same decision support capabilities, then it would be much amenable for the researcher to empirically contrast the impacts of F-T-F versus distributed meetings in group problem solving than those of non-GDSS versus GDSS.

10.2 RESEARCH DESIGN

10.2.1 Hypotheses

Based on the premise that recent developments in GDSS tools would increase the efficiency and effectiveness of group decision-making and problem-solving activities (Huber, 1984), the goal of the experiment was to focus in determining in which setting, distributed and face-to-face, a

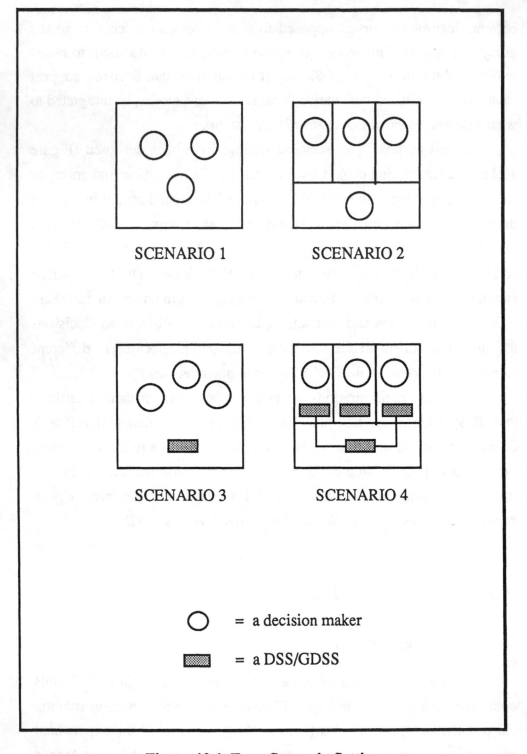

**Figure 10.1 Four Scenario Settings
(distributed vs. centralized and GDSS vs. non-GDSS)**

GDSS configuration would be more effective for high task and low relationship problems. In other words, this experiment sought to validate quadrant II shown in Figure 9.2 in two different settings: scenarios 3 and 4 of Figure 10.1. To determine the impact of GDSS on the decision making process, four hypotheses were tested using three decision-outcomes variables (decision quality, decision speed and user satisfaction), and a questionnaire. Since the Co-oP allows a new medium of group decision making, i.e., in distributed mode, the null hypotheses were formulated as follows:

H1: *Decision quality will be better in a distributed mode than in a face-to-face mode.*

For this experiment, decision quality was measured by four decision outcomes variables from the computer printouts of the group inputs and solutions: (1) number of original/creative criteria generated during the group solution process, (2) number of baseline criteria generated by the groups, (3) number of groups meeting the baseline criteria, and (4) the correct answer.

H2: *Distributed groups will require less man-minutes than face-to-face group to come up with a group solution.*

Read times, input times, and resulting total times were measured to ascertain the truth of the above hypothesis. Timing started once the case study had been issued. The time taken to read was the read time, the time to absorb and analyze the case was considered the input time, and the total time the sum of the two.

H3: *The decision satisfaction of the group members will be greater in the distributed mode than in the face-to-face mode.*

Four questions from a participant questionnaire, using a five-point Likert scale, were used to test this hypothesis. These included (1) satisfaction with the final results that the individual/group derived from their inputs, (2) satisfaction with the individual/group solution when compared to the expert's solution, (3) satisfaction with the number of criteria generated, and (4) preference for either F-T-F or distributed settings.

H4: *Participants will have no preference for either distributed settings or non-distributed settings.*

Given that both groups (i) used the same computer-mediated tool, (ii) worked on the same intellectual task requiring group members to work in a cooperative environment, and (iii) had a case with an answer that could be derived individually, it is presumed there would be no preference for either settings. Responses to the questionnaire were examined to determine answers to two questions: (a) Which type of setting will each group prefer? and (b) Are there significant enough differences between the two types of settings to state that one group clearly preferred one type of setting to the other?

10.2.2 Research Settings

The GDSS hardware in the experiment consisted of a decision laboratory specially designed for computer-based group decision making. The laboratory included several independent decision rooms served by a network of microcomputers with Co-oP installed in the server. Electronic mail, notepad and memory-resident calculator were also made available.

In order to insulate the subjects from encountering with technical difficulties, a facilitator was provided to each decision group. The facilitator role ranged from being a simple chauffeur, who operated the GDSS hardware and interfaced with the software during the group meetings, to being on call when the group experienced technical difficulties.

10.2.3 Subjects

Three criteria were considered for the identification, screening and selection of subjects: (i) the backgrounds and skills of participants, (ii) the logistics of setting up the experiment, and (iii) the number of subjects and/or group size. Thirty six officer-graduate students were selected, most of whom were from the Computer Systems Management curriculum at the Naval Postgraduate School, Monterey. All had served a minimum of five years as managers with a wide range of backgrounds. Moreover, as the fifth quarter students of a six quarter curriculum, all had been exposed to various management and MIS courses. As a group, they formed a relatively homogeneous group of participants, sharing comparative management experience and educational backgrounds, and thus, avoiding most of the noise associated with random subject selection (Fedorowicz et al., 1986). More important, participants knew one another in a manner suggestive of a corporate environment where groups of decision makers often have had the opportunity to work together.

10.2.4 Group Decision Task

A case study in management — i.e., the selection of a regional director for an overseas branch — primarily designed for testing group member interaction was chosen for the experiment. The case could be classified in Quadrant II of Figure 9.2 in that the solution to the task was assumed to be not too intuitively obvious at the outset, but rather required some degree of analysis and comparison of candidate attributes. Also the case was written in such a way that it minimizes the impact of interpersonal relationships on the group outcome.

Furthermore, the case was chosen based on its documented acceptability as a group problem-solving exercise, and on its face validity, supportability, content validity and external validity.

1. *Face validity*: Personnel selection is a situation often encountered in organizations. Sufficient information was provided to participants via candidate summary sheets to enable them to select the best candidate for the job. Also, expert's choice was readily available to evaluate subjects' decisions.

2. *Supportability*: Supportability implies the task at hand must lend itself to support by a GDSS. Co-oP has various decision methods that can support the personnel selection problem using multiple criteria decision models (e.g., A.H.P. and ELECTRE) and voting algorithms. The majority of subjects felt the GDSS used supported the test case well to very well.

3. *Content validity*: No questions were posed to highlight any discrepancies in this area and no problems were cited by any of the participants as to the content validity. As such, the assumption was made that the requirement of content validity was met.

4. *External validity*: External validity refers to how well the test case represent an actual decision-making situation in an organization. The majority of subjects responding to the questionnaire chose agree to strongly agree to express that the case had actual value.

10.2.5 Pretesting

Since the case study had been used successfully in previous experimental studies and the Co-oP software has reached its final phase of the development cycle, pretesting before initial administration was minimal. The pretesting was informally conducted by the debriefing method. Several management faculty members and students participated in the pretest. They were asked to report on any problem found with the case, the software and the questionnaire. Minor modifications were requested for both the questionnaire and the Co-oP user interface.

10.3 RESULTS AND DISCUSSION

The results of the experiment which address the hypotheses are discussed below: (See Table 10.1)

10.3.1 Decision Quality

(1) Number of original/creative criteria generated:
The possibility that F-T-F groups would generate a greater number of original and creative criteria, due to the exchange of ideas present in a non-distributed setting, was examined. The original/creative variable was measured base on the total number of criteria generated by each group. This total included the baseline criteria and any others mentioned during the test. The analysis of the results indicated that there was no difference between the groups across the two types of settings in formulating more original/creative criteria.

(2) Number of baseline criteria generated by each group
The number of baseline criteria generated by each group was analyzed using the computer printouts from the individual group sessions. To determine whether the individuals/groups correctly generated and met the baseline criteria, the weights assigned to each candidate for the position were carefully scrutinized. This was necessary since some individuals/groups came up with the right criteria, but incorrectly applied

H1: *Decision quality will be better in a distributed mode than in a face-to-face mode.*

NOT REJECTED.

H2: *Distributed groups will require less man-minutes to come up with a group solution.*

NOT REJECTED.

H3: *The decision satisfaction of the group members will be greater in distributed mode.*

INCONCLUSIVE.

H4: *Participants will have no preference for either non-distributed settings or distributed settings.*

H4a: *Which setting will each group prefer?*
For the face-to-face group: REJECTED.
For the distributed group : NOT REJECTED.

H4b: *Is there significant difference between the two settings to state one group clearly preferred on setting more than the other?*

NOT REJECTED.

Table 10.1. Summary of Experimental Results

them to the candidates. Only those correctly applied were credited for having successfully met the baseline criteria requirements. The analysis of the results showed that F-T-F groups generated more baseline criteria, but this had no effect on the quality of the final result. This was basically due to the weighing strategy employed by the groups.

(3) Number of groups meeting the baseline criteria:

Although the non-distributed groups meeting the baseline criteria was slightly larger, the difference was not statistically significant enough to state clearly which group generated and met the baseline criteria more often.

(4) Correct answer:

To determine which setting produced a greater number of correct answers, each group's final result was compared against the experts' answer. Four out of six distributed groups versus two out of six F-T-F groups had the correct solution. Since the distributed groups scored 50% better, F-T-F groups were clearly less effective.

To summarize, the only decision quality measure that showed a clear distinction between the two settings in this experiment was the number of correct answers derived by the groups. As stated above, distributed groups were clearly more effective.

10.3.2 Decision Speed

The actual time taken by the groups, while deriving a solution, constituted the second area for data analysis. Read times, input times, and resulting totals were recorded to demonstrate that distributed groups would require less man-hours to reach the solution. The read times showed a significant difference between the F-T-F and distributed groups. On the other hand, F-T-F groups spent less time in the read phase than did distributed groups.

F-T-F groups spent more time in the input phase and, therefore, expended more time overall deriving a solution. On the average, each individual member of the F-T-F groups spent 46.2 minutes; whereas, individual members of distributed groups spent 25.8 minutes in the process. As a result, F-T-F groups were much less efficient. This is to be expected, since individuals can make decisions much more quickly than groups by bypassing discussions.

10.3.3 Satisfaction Level

Responses to the questionnaire were used to measure the differences in satisfaction level between the two settings. The results suggested that members of distributed groups were 'satisfied' to 'very satisfied' with their final individual result.

Only 50% of distributed group members were 'satisfied' with their final group result; whereas, 67% of the F-T-F groups were 'satisfied'. The results also showed that both group members were 'satisfied' to 'very satisfied' with their individual/group solution when compared to the experts' solution. Finally, data indicated no difference in the satisfaction level between the two groups.

10.3.4 Setting Preference

Since this experiment was conducted using two distinct settings, the participants were asked which setting they preferred. The premise was that there would be no preference for either setting. The distributed groups' mean value was slightly above the population mean; however, the difference was not significant enough to state clearly that a preference for F-T-F setting existed. However, F-T-F groups significantly preferred the non-distributed setting. This preference may be due to the fact that the subjects have had extensive managerial training and experience in dealing with F-T-F communications whereas distributed decision making were not conventional to them.

SUMMARY

This chapter reported the results of a experimental study that sought to determine in which setting — distributed and face-to-face — a GDSS such as Co-oP would be more effective.

Given the case study and the current features of Co-oP, it was found that distributed groups had better decision quality and faster decision speed than the F-T-F groups during the decision-making process. The conclusion is that for the task chosen, subjects in the distributed groups utilized Co-oP more effectively and efficiently. However, the question as to whether the subjects of one group were more satisfied with their solutions and final group results than the other group cannot be answered conclusively.

Given the rapid advancements in the communication and computer technologies coupled with the increasing pressure to resolve with more frequent and complex decisions, it is expected that organizations will use distributed computer-mediated communication systems by organizations. The results found in this study suggested that the distributed mode of group problem solving is not only a viable alternative but also a promising decision-making process.

Additional studies are needed to expand the results presented in this studies. These studies can take a number of directions. First, the research design in this study can be replicated to compare scenarios 1-and-3 and 2-and-4. Also, the use different types of experimental case studies could help further gain insight into the use and impact of a GDSS on organizational decision making.

11. NON-COOPERATION IN GDSS

As the number of GDSS implementation and uses increase, informal experience and early evaluation, such as the one reported in the previous chapter, continue to show the usefulness of GDSS in cooperative settings. Bass (1983) argues that the lack of sufficient cooperation is often a determining factor that prevents the group from reaching satisfactory results. Is it possible to create GDSS for non-cooperation? If yes, how can it be effective used? This chapter attempts to shed some insights to these two questions and to explore some design issues for building GDSS for non-cooperation environments (Bui, Jarke and Shakun, 1987).

11.1 NON-COOPERATION IN GROUP DECISION MAKING

As defined earlier, in a cooperative decision-making situation, the group members attempt to reach a common decision in a friendly and trusting manner, and share the responsibility for that decision. In the non-cooperative decision situation, the decision makers play the role of adversaries or disputants. Common forms of non-cooperative decision making often originate as conflict and competition. While the former represents a situation in which disputants seek to impair their opponents to pursue their own interest, the latter is characterized by the fact that each competitor actively attempts to outperform each other. Non-cooperative situations are often plagued with varying levels of mistrust, misrepresentation of facts, incomplete information exchange, attempt to outperform or even hurt others, and sometimes, with the unwillingness to resolve the collective problem.

11.1.1 Conflicts as Causes of Non-cooperation

As decision makers struggle for a mutually acceptable option, differences among them in perceptions, cognition, values, interests and needs give rise to conflicts. One can identify a number of sources of conflict.

First, conflict exists whenever interaction by multiple decision makers uniquely affects their respective environments, and the nature of their interaction is such that it is impossible for all involved parties to achieve their desired goals (Kahan and Rapaport, 1984). In a MCDM context, Zeleny (1982) defines conflict as when multiple distinct strategies, selected as the means of achieving goals or objectives, are *mutually exclusive* and when available alternatives, when considered separately, are capable of satisfying only a portion or a particular aspect of a goal. Implicit in the troublesome interaction process between multiple decision makers is the *coalition* problem. Coalitions are alliances of group members combining their individual powers, resources and persuasive efforts to enforce greater influence on decision processes than the members could accomplish alone. Coalitions are commonly observed when conflicting interests are present in a group. Whenever three or more group members get together to jointly resolve a problem of common interest to them, it is likely that at least two of them will at some point in time unite forces to their mutual advantage.

Second, the very existence of an organization is another source of conflict because of the inherent nature of the organizational decision making process. The organizational information flows follow a grid of communications made up of conflicting channels (Bass, 1983). The decision needs to be accepted by those responsible for authorizing and implementing it and often fails to satisfy all decision criteria.

Disagreement about means or ends constitute a third source of conflict. Organizations find it difficult to allocate scarce resources. The allocation process often creates turmoil within corporate ranks since the attempt at optimality may reduce 'slack' throughout the organization. This reduction may not be seen as beneficial by individual groups, with this slack regarded as necessary buffers for dealing with future uncertainties. This allocation process is further clouted by the managerial tendency to overemphasize the achievement of immediate or short-term goals at the expense of future or long-term ones.

Finally, change — or more precisely, resistance to change — is a source of conflict. Innovative alternatives to entrenched policies are often seen by organizations as dangerous and not considered in any methodical and rational way.

11.1.2 General Approaches to Deal with Conflicts

Zeleny (1982) delineates neglect, containment, control and denial as four *attitudes* of dealing with conflict. A group member may neglect or disregard a conflict and implements his own decisions. He can contain conflict by 'freezing' it to gain time and let things cool off. Also, he may attempt to control conflict by adding constraints that limit the problem solving process or eventually the decision outcomes. Denying the existence of conflict refers to the process of acknowledging only the existence of a certain situation, but then advancing a different interpretation. Persuasion, propaganda, and even brainwashing, are means to conflict denial.

From the *outcome* perspective, Ackoff (1978) describes three methods for dealing with conflict: solution, resolution, and dissolution. Solving a conflict is the search of a single and acceptable solution. One may prescriptively accept the factors that induced the conflict, only to do whatever is necessary to obtain the best outcome one can. For example, a decision maker might try to solve a strike, by outwardly accepting it, and then closing the plant down.

The resolution of conflict is the subject of numerous unilateral and multilateral methodologies to reach the ideal outcomes for all parties including negotiation, bargaining and arbitration. Higher authority and great power may be engaged to resolve a conflict, or the conflict may be settled adaptively in a collective manner utilizing negotiation and bargaining. Bass (1983) argues that mediators and arbitrators may be employed to proposed a mutually advantageous solution, one that is agreeable to all parties and nearly optimal. Such a solution can be found by integrating conflicting interests rather than by merely attempting to compromise one side over the other. Finally, dissolving a conflict is a common strategy to completely remove the conflict. However this often results in further conflict.

11.1.3 Search for a More Cooperative Environment

Regardless of the group members' attitudes or the group approach to handle conflict, research on the social psychology of conflict emphasizes the value of striving cooperatively rather than with a competitive motivation (Douglas, 1962; Morley and Stephenson, 1977). Such a notion stresses the importance of shifting from an initial competitive (or even hostile) stage to a more cooperative one (Kochan and Jick, 1978). Ideally, group problem solving in a non-cooperative environment should be characterized by a gradually evolving, cooperative search for mutually acceptable, equitable, and innovative solutions with which the group members feel that their individual objectives are met rather than scoring a 'victory' over the others. While each party will actively protect and advance its own interests, this should be done with a view to seeking arrangements that will satisfy the other parties as well. Furthermore, when there is a mediator, maintaining a cooperative orientation also applies to this person.

11.2 GROUP DECISION SUPPORT IN A NON-COOPERATIVE SETTING

The assumption that the adoption of a cooperative orientation is a key to a constructive conflict resolution, leads to the concept that non-cooperation is a generalization of cooperative decision making. Therefore, from a system design point of view, it would make a great deal of sense to build non-cooperative Group Decision Support Systems (GDSS) in such a way that they can help transform a competitive problem into a cooperative one. When successful, such a system could be a major step towards more effective group decision making in a less restricted setting than hitherto possible.

At least three additional design considerations should be envisioned:

- *Focus on negotiation and settlement support:* Supporting a non-cooperative situation can refer to the manner in which the GDSS facilitates the achievement of a constructive group problem solving. Criteria for an effective non-cooperative settlement process can be defined by the following (Blake, 1979; Deutsch, 1973; Pruitt, 1981):

  — resolution of all relevant issues;

  — technically correct agreements expressed in clear, unambiguous language;

  — agreements that are fair and equitable relative to prevailing norms;

  — creative agreements searching for new opportunities that are beneficial to both parties;

— satisfaction with the overall results;

— parties comply with their terms of the agreements; and

— parties are better able to cooperate.

- *Emphasis on the behavioral process:* The GDSS should facilitate behavioral processes rather than just help the decision makers attack tasks. The GDSS must be used as a means to build trust and confidence. Among specific tactics which may foster a sense of trust and confidence are explicit statements of reassurance, the judicious use of self-disclosure and the maintenance of confidentiality. The outcome of such an effort is to reach a mutually informed commitment to the recourse to a GDSS as a mediation process. Such an emphasis on the behavioral process can be achieved by providing the following capabilities:

— Cooperative orientation to the group members in such a way that the parties define their task as a cooperative effort to achieve mutual or compatible goals and avoid pseudo-issues that are merely a bargaining ploy to gain leverage over opponents (Rubin and Brown, 1975). Common interests and similarities are highlighted, while downplaying opposite interests and values.

— An 'open' style of communication implies active, mutual participation in the give-and-take of negotiating.

— Search for reasonable and persuasive goals that are well-focused and achievable enough to resolve conflicts.

- *Facilitating the tasks of the mediator:* Recourse to a human mediator (or some sort of external agent) may increase the degree of acceptance of the GDSS as a novel channel of collective decision making. An effective GDSS for non-cooperation decision making should help the mediator accomplish this difficult task. When the role of the mediator is strongly disliked by one or more members, then the mediator — and probably the GDSS — may no longer be feasible. The issues here are how well the mediator can use the GDSS to maintain confidentiality and, when necessary, disclose information. The GDSS must support the mediator in educating himself about the nature of the problem. In particular, the GDSS should help the mediator accurately diagnose the following aspects:

  — The prevalence of group member misdiagnosis. The sources of misdiagnosis may include incomplete information;

  — The multiple viewpoints of the problem;

  — The group member's understanding of the role of the mediator. The mediator should have the possibility to access to other sources of information to expand his understanding.

11.3 DESIGN SPECIFICATIONS FOR GDSS COMPONENTS

After addressing some general requirements for GDSS in a non-cooperative setting, we now turn to specific issues concerning the design of the four GDSS components.

11.3.1 Communications and User Interface Managers

The design objective is to create a computer-based environment favorable for constructive problem solving. Three tasks can be envisaged. The first and most crucial one is a thorough orientation to persuade the potential GDSS user about the nature and purpose of using the GDSS as a fair mediation tool. The second is to manage ambivalence. The third is to 'socialize' the users into the appropriate norms. The rationale and motivation of these tasks are given below:

- Goal-oriented or outcome-oriented group members are more disposed to encourage a 'state of harmony' than a 'state of disharmony'. The communications component should tune the group members to a problem-oriented state. When focusing on problem solving, members are expected to become more tolerant of group differences since they can be convinced that mutual acceptance is necessary for the good of the group.

- Equal participation in defining collective intentions and actions have proven important in eliciting a common problem. The GDSS should be built in such a way that it promotes equal participation in constructing the group norm by widening the spectrum of communications support (both formal and informal).

- The process of building a computer-based group norm should be flexible enough to reflect the collective decision-making structure, including power structure and possible formation of constructive coalitions.

11.3.2 Data Manager

Research on cooperative work using shared databases, e.g., in computer-aided design (Klahold et al., 1985; Bancilhon et al., 1985) has recognized a number of issues many of which are also relevant to GDSS design. Non-cooperative decision making, adds some additional problems to this list:

- *Locking mechanism:* In a multiple user environment, group members access data simultaneously. This may lead to a situation in which two or more users access that same data item while others are attempting to alter it. This concurrency problem is particularly prevalent in a non-cooperative environment in that the search for orientation and understanding require a lot of data transfer. Also, since data requests are often short but frequent, the data manager must have quick locking mechanisms that enable locking data items before access, or validating a transaction after its completion. While such mechanisms are standard in mainframe DBMS, they are still missing in many micro-based systems.

- *Partial ordering on the access of transaction:* Differences in users' skills lead to the need for knowledge sharing via user-to-user communication. To keep track of information exchange and sharing, the data component should include partial ordering on the data access by transaction.

- *Filtering/sorting/time stamping mechanisms:* Such procedures highlight differences in opinion.

- *Distributed and/or sub-databases:* Transfer of individual files to group databases or between individual files should be possible.

- *Procedure to enforce privacy:* Privacy enforcement mechanisms should be made available to all members.

- Communications using extended integrating rules to turn on/off links with *external databases*.

The relative importance of these items vary from situation to situation.

11.3.3 Model Component

Voting procedures and other techniques of aggregation of preferences are common forms of collective decision making. In a non-cooperative decision-making situation, emphasis should be on techniques that (i) search areas of consensus or compromise, (ii) identify feasible and acceptable collective goals, (iii) explore novel options, and (iv) enhance effective communications (i.e., help group members organize their thoughts and communicate them effectively). As a framework for such models, a concept of evolutionary system design (Shakun 1981a, 1981b, 1987; Jarke et al., 1986) and search for compromise (Bui and Shakun, 1987) have proven useful.

11.4 FACTORS INHIBITING THE USE OF A GDSS

As mentioned earlier, a GDSS is expected to be successful principally in certain kinds of non-cooperative decision situations. In this section, four factors which may prevent success of a GDSS are addressed. This may also circumscribe situations where emphasis on human intervention might be more effective:

(1) *High level of intra-party conflict:* If one of the parties is ambivalent about the problem to be solved or about the desirability of dealing openly and fairly with other parties, it is plausible that he may not wish to use a GDSS. Group member's ambivalence about using a GDSS may derive from conscious or unconscious wishes to attack rather than to negotiate, from fears of becoming vulnerable because of the other's greater negotiating skills or resources, and from ignorance of the goals and methods of the mediator. While the last two possible sources could be remedied by the GDSS Group Norm Constructor and an appropriate Help facility, gaining the crucial cooperation of a group member is beyond the capability of the GDSS. More important, the ambivalence generated by one party can spread and intensify quickly to others.

(2) *Well-established, rigid patterns of destructive interaction:* Studies of labor mediation reveal that the worse the state of the parties' relationship with one another and the more intense their conflict, the dimmer the prospects for effective mediation. While a GDSS is less apt to be perceived as partial or biased than the human counterpart, its use in a intense and long-standing conflict can be minimal although not harmful. The distributed GDSS can be transformed into a disconnected set of individual DSS. The group decision support is then concentrated on the individual level including the one of the mediator.

(3) *Scarcity of divisible resources:* When resources are scarce, trade-offs among parties become difficult if not impossible. This obstacle is however independent of the role of GDSS with the exception that the GDSS can be used to help redefine the problem to lessen this uneven distribution of scarce resources.

(4) *Unbalance or disparities in relative bargaining power:* When there is unbalance in relative bargaining power, the stronger party is likely to be less motivated to compromise and more likely to use intransigent tactics. Meanwhile, the less powerful party may react with passive concession or reactive defiance (Deutsch, 1973; Rubin and Brown, 1975). Such an ill-matched confrontation does not constitute a sound basis for settlement (Kressel, 1981). Using GDSS to solve differences may not work. However, GDSS for individual negotiation support could remain very helpful for any of the party involved.

SUMMARY

Assuming that a basic approach to effective non-cooperative problem solving is to restore the trust and confidence of the parties, a fundamental mission of a GDSS is to reduce resistance to use the system as a channel or medium for resolving a collective problem. Attaining this can sometimes be difficult. A GDSS in a non-cooperative environment as opposed to a cooperative environment should (i) seek and maintain acceptability (ii) while simultaneously intervening to reduce hostilities and effectuate a more promising interpersonal climate. The Group Norm Constructor discussed in this book (Section 8.4) can be used to implement an array of tactics to separate the parties, invoke norms of cooperation and fair play, interrupting dysfunctional or hostile exchanges, educate the parties about their mutual role in negative transactions, invoke their mutual interest in solving the collective problems, and so on.

Since the ability of the parties to cooperate with one another is the primary predictor of a successful outcome, the use of a GDSS seems appropriate for parties for whom a ambience of cooperation already exists or where the prospects of developing it quickly are relatively good. The recourse to a GDSS for a joint problem-solving venture should make sense to all involved parties.

Under certain circumstances, GDSS could be used as a appropriate means to handle non-cooperative problems. They constitute a promising adjunct to the exclusive use of human mediation in orchestrating a constructive group decision-making process. Benefits derived from using GDSS may include improvement of communication, understanding, and ultimately, problem settlement.

More research is needed before we can be confident that attempts to build GDSS for negotiation are fruitful. Is the process of designing non-cooperative GDSS germane to a human and formal negotiation? May it be equally or more helpful in this respect than non-GDSS mediation (or better than inexperienced mediators)? For what types of parties is what communications norms most likely to be helpful? What are the criteria to distinguish a 'cooperative' context from a 'non-cooperative' one? How to identify obstacles that stand in the way of achieving a constructive settlement? What GDSS intervention strategies are the most useful?

12. GDSS DESIGN FOR ORGANIZATIONAL DECISION-MAKING

To date, most DSS have been designed to support individual decision makers, and as discussed so far, groups of decision makers. GDSS in their present architecture take little cognizance of the fact that decision makers are influenced by their organizational and societal context inside as well as outside their working group. Despite their use of electronic media to facilitate and control information exchange among users, they provide little information regarding organizational elements for executive use. Thus, it seems important to explore issues of expanding GDSS to organizational DSS, in particular the ones that addresses the following questions: (i) What are the factors that distinguish existing individual and group decision support systems from DSS for organizational decision making? (ii) How can GDSS be extended to include some of these factors into the decision support environment? In addressing these questions, this chapter follows a three-step discussion. First, it reviews four major models of organizational decision making addressed in the management literature. Second, its uses a MCDM framework to cross compare these models. Third, it applies the Entity-Relationship approach to identify the major entities addressed in the four models as well as their interrelationships (Bui and Jarke, 1987).

The model proposed in this chapter can be used to (i) provide a framework for the analysis and design of organizational DSS, complementary to the more process-oriented approach (e.g., Meador, Guyote and Rosenfeld, 1986), (ii) allow the classification of existing DSS and related systems such as DBMS or expert systems in terms of their organizational coverage, (iii) enable the identification of opportunities for new kinds of DSS, and (iv) to permit the study of various possible decompositions of the organizational decision processes (e.g., task reapportionment between man and machine defined by Fjeldstad and Konsynski, 1986).

12.1 A DEFINITION OF ORGANIZATIONAL DSS

An organizational DSS can be defined as a computer-based system that attempts to support organizational decisions. Research on organizational decision making often differentiates three levels of decision situations: decision making by one person, by a group of persons, and by groups of persons affiliated with one or more organizations. In an organizational context, DSS users play the role of chauffeurs or intermediaries. As intermediaries, decision makers may no longer be the end nodes of the computer-based interaction scheme. Rather, the organization becomes the ultimate end of the interaction chain (Figure 12.1). Consequently, factors that characterize and dictate organizational decision making should be included in the architecture of GDSS.

12.2 ORGANIZATIONAL DECISION MAKING AND MCDM

Virtually, all individual DSS are in one way or another based on Simon's decision-making model which comprises the major steps of intelligence, design, and choice. In contrast, there seems to be no general agreement on an organizational decision model. At least four basic classes of models must be mentioned: (i) the program /bureaucratic model, (ii) the rational choice model, (iii) the political model, and (iv) the cybernetic/garbage can model.

The *program/bureaucratic* model assumes that organizations are stable and predictable. Only standardized procedures are needed to prevent the organization from deviating from its preset goals (Simon, 1957; Crozier, 1964; Mintzberg, 1971).

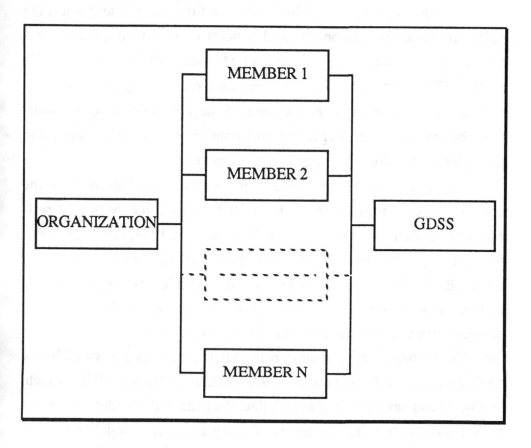

Figure 12.1. DSS Users as Intermediaries

The *rational choice* approach refers to analytical tools that iteratively search for optimal solutions using maximization techniques proposed by theories of cause-and-effect relations (Popper, 1959; March and Simon, 1958; Downs, 1966; Simon, 1969; Allison, 1970; Mintzberg, Raisinghani, and Theoret, 1976). Economic models best illustrate this approach

(Savage, 1954; Luce and Raiffa, 1958; Stigler, 1961; Marschak, 1955; Radner and Rothschild, 1975). While they are useful in solving well-defined and deterministic problems, experience has proven that they are not appropriate when dealing with ill-structured situations (Lindblom, 1959; Cyert and March, 1963; Tversky and Kahneman, 1974; Williamson, 1975).

Recognizing the practical limitations of the rational framework, the *political* model focuses on political aspects of various organizational constituencies (March, 1962; Hills and Mahoney, 1978; Perrow, 1979; Pfeffer, 1981). Political maps are identified to achieve goals of various constituencies, perhaps at the expense of the organization as a whole. Distribution of power, bargaining and conflict resolution are common strategies adopted for regulating the organization.

Cybernetic procedures relate outcomes to the objectives of the decision-makers through the imitation of choices, feedback and self-correction (Wiener, 1948; Ashby, 1952; Lindblom, 1959; Forrester, 1961; Steinbruner, 1974; Beer, 1975). This consists of search and selection of any available solution that worked for a similar problem before, by focusing on past instances where beneficial outcomes were observed and avoiding solution strategies that had resulted in negative outcomes.

Yet another decision strategy is the random strategy advocated by the *garbage can model* (Cohen et al., 1972; March and Olsen, 1976; March, 1978). Under severe lack of knowledge, decision makers adopt a random search and choice rule. Variations of the garbage can model have been investigated by (Padgett, 1980; Sabrosky, et al., 1982; Anderson and Fisher, 1984; Carley, 1984).

Figure 12.2 contrasts the four organizational models according to their philosophical premises, decision processes, information requirements, model requirements, and decision outcomes. As mentioned above, each of these models, or any combination of them, could be the most appropriate one, depending on the decisions to be supported. However, the combined use of such models in a DSS framework requires a generic representation.

	RATIONAL CHOICE	POLITICAL COMPETITIVE	PROGRAM/ BUREAUCRATIC	GARBAGE CAN/ CYBERNETIC
Philosophy Premises	Organization effectiveness/ efficiency (optimization)	Organization sub-optimi-zation	Stability/ Predictability (programmin correctness)	Problem solving (search for opportunities)
Decision Processes	Normative procedures/ substantive rationality	Procedural rationality/ conflict resolution	Standardized procedures	Ad-hoc
Information Requirements	Systematic, complete	Extensive staging	Historical, accurate, timely	Random
Model Requirements	Analytical Support	Dynamic/3rd party interven.	Extrapolation	Multi-purpose model/timing
Decision Outcome	Optimal Solution	Settlement/ Power distr.	Norms, job design, rewards	Interactions of problem solution
Examples	O.R., simu-lation of org. environment	Organizational structure		Consensus

Figure 12.2. Characteristics of Four Organizational Decision Making Models

In this chapter, we choose the structure of multiple criteria decision models as such a generic representation.

The choice of MCDM as a generic representation can be justified as follows (see also Bui, 1984). First of all, it appears obvious that an organizational DSS should be a group DSS. Each of the four models implies participation of multiple parties in the decision process even though the assumptions about their role differ substantially. As argued by Keen (1977) and demonstrated by research efforts done with Co-oP, MCDM have proven to provide an elegant framework in:

- *representing multiple viewpoints of a problem:* From a database perspective, the MCDM decision matrix can be viewed as a particular kind of derived relation whose rows represent decision alternatives and whose columns represent criteria or viewpoints by which the alternatives are evaluated;

- *aggregating the preferences of multiple decision makers according to various group norms:* MCDM and game theory have developed different weighing schemes for criteria and measures of 'fairness' for multiperson decisions;

- *organizing the decision process:* Dynamic game theory (Crawford, 1985) and interactive MCDM have recognized that preferences of decision makers are not necessarily rigid. They may not even exist a priori but are formed during the decision process itself; a typical procedure consisting of problem definition, group constitution, prioritization of evaluation criteria, determination of individual preferences, aggregation of individual preferences, and evolution of individual and group preferences through consensus-seeking and compromise (negotiation) emerged.

Beyond this general argument, it can also be shown that the specific concepts inherent in each of the models can be represented in the MCDM framework. For each model, Figure 12.3 presents a summary of typical questions or issues using the four major stages of multiple criteria decision making. In the bureaucratic model, MCDM supports hierarchical decomposition of goals set for the organization. In the rational choice model, MCDM helps determine an optimal solution under a well-defined set of multiple objectives and constraints. In the political model where the presence of multiple decision makers is predominant, MCDM can facilitate consensus seeking and compromise by introducing multiple negotiation aspects. Finally, the garbage can type of decision making can use MCDM for ad-hoc situation assessment and selection of choice policies under uncertainty.

12.3 AN ENTITY-RELATIONSHIP MODEL

As previously argued, MCDM concepts seem to be appropriate for capturing the organizational decision-making process and, make it amenable to the introduction of DSS concepts. However, concrete organizational entities and their interrelationships in a MCDM-based DSS have yet to be identified. This section maps the structure of organizational decision making onto an abstract data model. This model can be used as a basis for organizational DSS design. Once made available, such a data model could make it possible to evaluate the capabilities and limitations of current DSS in terms of the problems and contextual factors they address.

The representational framework we use is the Entity-Relationship model proposed by Chen (1976). This approach has proven useful in analyzing and designing complex business-oriented systems (e.g., Stohr, 1980). The model presented in this paper attempts:

	RATIONAL CHOICE	POLITICAL COMPETITIVE	PROGRAM/ BUREAUCRATIC	GARBAGE CAN/ CYBERNETIC
Search for alternatives	What are the strategies that lead to effectiveness and efficicency?	What are the tactics that reveal favorable for each of the parties involved?	What are the programs that minimize mysfunctional routines?	What are the solutions and/or the opportunities?
Assessment of a consistent family of criteria	What are the organizational objectives?	What are the objectives of each of the involved parties?	What are the elements that characterize the routinization?	What are the impacts of the solutions?
Assessment of preferences	What are the decision makers' preferences?	Who are involved? What are the differences in prioritization of objectives?	What are the organizational priorities?	What are the expert's judgments on the solutions?
Utilization of interactive method to find a compromise solution	Composite ranking, vector of pay-offs	What are the rules that could resolve or dissolve conflicts?	multi-objective linear programming	Tables of Probabilities and opportunities

Figure 12.3.   Organizational Decision Making Models and MCDM processes

(1) To capture *semantic information* about the organizational context that surrounds the decision process; and thus, to identify DSS requirements for expanding Group DSS to support organizational decision making.

(2) To support the selection of DSS tools for *different types* of organizational decision situations.

Figure 12.4 exhibits an Entity-Relationship diagram of organizational decision making, thus revealing possible roles of MCDM-based DSS in an organizational context. The entities represent the elements that intervene in a decision-making process, whereas the relationships describe how these elements interact with each other. By convention, entities are presented by rectangles and relationships by diamonds. The rationale of the entity sets is discussed first. Then, the relationships among these entities will be studied.

12.3.1 The Organizational Decision-Making Entities

The entities of the model can be partitioned into three groups. The upper two entities in Figure 12.4 (ACCESSIBLE REAL WORLD, KNOWN WORLD) represent the environment relevant to the decision. The three entities in the middle (DECISION ALTERNATIVES, EXPECTED REAL WORLD, EVALUATION CRITERIA) derive from structuring the decision problem in terms of MCDM. The lower three entities model the actors in organizational decision processes. We now describe each of these entities in some detail.

E1. *ACCESSIBLE REAL WORLD:* This entity represents all the states of the world accessible by some specific means, including those not currently known to the decision makers. The purpose of this entity set is twofold:

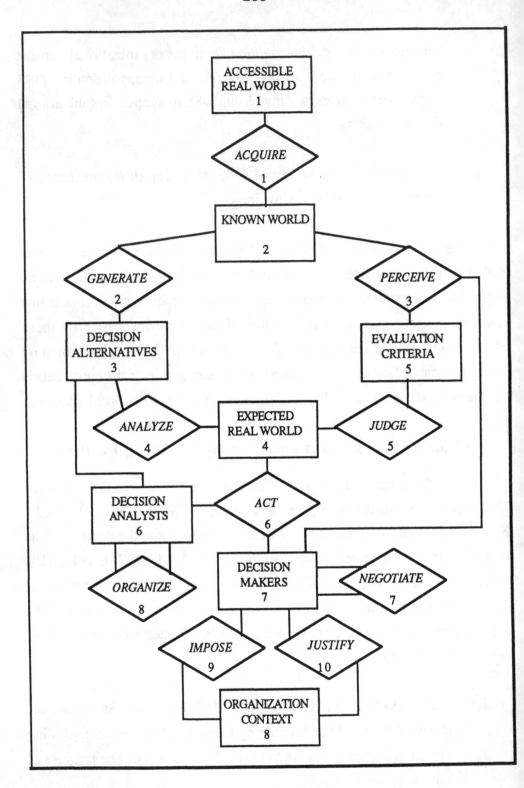

**Figure 12.4.   An Entity-Relationship Model
for Organization DSS**

(i)   To ensure the 'openness' of the DSS. Experience has shown that the design of an open system, as opposed to a closed system, is crucial to the capture of the dynamics and complexity of the decision situations (Beer, 1975; Van Aken, 1982);

(ii)   To determine the boundaries of the environment beyond which the accessible real world is no longer relevant to the decision situation.

Examples of this entity type include the 'boundary spanners' and the 'gatekeepers'. Mintzberg (1973), Aldrich and Hecker (1977) cite the decision maker's subordinates, business associates as typical examples of boundary spanners. Conversely, the gatekeepers are the constituencies that are reluctant to disseminate information (Galbraith, 1977).

E2.   *KNOWN WORLD:* This entity includes all the states of the world that the decision makers are aware of. This constitutes the set of raw information that will be transformed into a source of operational information of the decision analysis. Corporate documentation, data bases or knowledge bases in Expert Systems are examples of this entity type.

E3.   *DECISION ALTERNATIVES:* All relevant courses of action that are potentially able to entirely or partially resolve a given problem. The existence of this entity ensures the viability of the decision situation. Decision alternatives are often defined in forms of strategies, tactics, projects. For a given decision problem, alternatives may be different depending on the three decision phases: pre-decision, decision and post-decision. For example,

Go/No-Go (i.e., status quo), and Now/Later (i.e., delay) are three special types of alternatives often considered in the post-decision phase.

E4. *EXPECTED REAL WORLD:* Alternatives or courses of action are meaningless to the decision makers unless they provide some values to them. This entity set conveys to the decision makers the expected or likely consequences that potential alternatives provide and will provide (Tversky and Kahneman, 1986).

E5. *EVALUATION CRITERIA:* This entity set translates the decision maker(s)' selected evaluation references into independent evaluation criteria. The latter will make it possible to compare alternatives. Profitability, growth, and personal satisfaction are common evaluation criteria. Rockart's Critical Success Factors provide examples of the Evaluation Criteria Set (Rockart, 1979; Sanders et al, 1982).

E6. *DECISION MAKERS:* This entity set includes one or more persons who ultimately have the final word and are responsible for their decision making. The issue here is to identify the 'real' decision makers in order to support them. Examples of types of decision makers are Mason and Mitroff's Leibnitz-, Hegel-, and Kant-type of decision maker. Connolly (1977), Mintzberg (1971), and Simon (1967) are among numerous researchers who study the profiles of decision makers, although some aspects, especially cognitive style, have undergone severe criticism as a design guideline (Huber, 1983).

E7. *DECISION ANALYSTS:* This set refers to the decision experts or consultants whose aim is to assist the decision makers in the understanding of complex decision situation and the optimization of the use of decision aids (Roy, 1976).

E8. *ORGANIZATIONAL CONTEXT:* This entity set contains all organizational elements — i.e., environment, people, technology, structure — that impose constraints on the decision makers and, to a degree, the decision analysts. The existence of this set is crucial to differentiate organizational and non-organizational decision situations (Perrow, 1970; Miles and Snow, 1978; Crozier, 1964).

12.3.2 The Organizational Decision-Making Relationships

The relationships (diamonds) in Figure 12.4 describe activities in the organizational decision process. Broadly speaking, they can be categorized into several levels according to the stages of the multiple criteria decision procedure as described in section 12.2.

The upper three activities (ACQUIRE, GENERATE, PERCEIVE) correspond to the stages of problem recognition and problem structuring in terms of alternatives and criteria. The second level represents the study of decision outcomes and their evaluation by individual decision makers and analysts. The lower right of Figure 12.4 models the intragroup (NEGOTIATE) and intergroup (IMPOSE, JUSTIFY) interaction of decision makers, thus modelling the phases of preference aggregation, negotiation, and organizational implementation. Finally, the ORGANIZE activity refers to the meta-level organization of the whole decision process. A description of each relationship follows, along with a set of questions to be answered by a decision support component for this activity.

R1. **ACQUIRE:** One can recognize two broad classes of information acquisition: explosive and restricted. The purpose of the first class is to increase the boundaries of the known world by gathering additional information. The underlying assumption of this knowledge acquisition process is that the more information the decision-maker has, the more likely he can improve his decision performance. Conversely, the second class of acquisition consists of reducing the large amount of information already available to the decision maker. The aim of this downgrading or 'staging' process is to capture only a few, yet indispensable and most relevant decision elements.

The existence of the ACQUIRE relationship raises at least three important issues: (i) the search process (How can relevant information be found? Is the cost of search appropriate (Stigler, 1961)? Is the mode of accessing information slow or fast, public or private?); (ii) the storage process (How can one avoid information redundancy or overload that can lead to losses in predictive accuracy? (Kleinmuntz, 1975; Chesnut and Jacoby, 1982)), and (iii) the multi-dimensionality of information cues (How should cues be selected to filter information?).

R2. **GENERATE:** The generation of alternatives could be done in two modes, either sequentially (Fischoff, Slovic and Lichtenstein, 1978) or simultaneously. Feasibility, affordability, comparability, substitutability, and independence between alternatives are important factors in the generation process. Furthermore, the issues of completeness and frequency of (re-)generation of alternatives should be explored.

R3. *PERCEIVE:* The raison d'etre of this relationship is to give formal structure to the decision maker's preferences, goals and values by (i) filtering and condensing the perceived values, and by (ii) defining threshold values necessary to the start of the decision making process. The issues of the decision maker's intuition and attention have been extensively stressed in the behavioral literature on decision-making. How can intuition that plays the role of diagnosis (Mintzberg, Raisinghani and Theoret, 1976) be captured and made accessible to the computer? What induces the decision makers' attention or 'enactment' i.e., their perceived degree of relevance and not information per se (Simon, 1967; Weick, 1979).

R4. *ANALYZE:* This relationship focuses on the accurate interpretations of fact by extrapolating expected and eventually objective consequences that the alternatives might provide. Analytical tools such as OR/MS models, econometric and heuristic models could be used to perform this relationship. Unresolved issues that analytical tools often encounter can again be addressed here: How much time series data does one need to accurately estimate potential consequences of a given set of decision alternatives? Further, how does one define the time horizon or time lags of consequences?

R5. *JUDGE:* This relationship summarizes various techniques that allow the decision maker to express his personal judgment of the consequences that the alternatives might have. The issues here are numerous. Among these, how does one depict goal ambiguity, unsure or fuzzy preferences emotionally embedded in the decision maker's evaluation processes (March, 1978).

R6. *ACT:* This relationship refers to the use of decision techniques as vehicles to guide actions. In principle, all appropriate decision modes can belong to this relationship. Taking steps towards actions often means restricting the degree of freedom, by choosing or reducing the set of alternatives. This might lead to conflict in actions (Shephard, 1964) or sometimes to avoidance of confrontation (e.g., status quo, refusal, delay, inattention). The issues here are: What decision techniques should one choose? When should one switch from one technique to the other?

R7. *NEGOTIATE:* This relationship becomes relevant when the decision situation is characterized by more than one decision-maker. This set should leave room to the DSS builder to select and make use of appropriate multiple user decision models. These models can be derived from game theory (e.g., Heidel, 1980) or from behavioral research (e.g., Walton, 1969).

R8. *IMPOSE:* This relationship stresses the important impact of different elements of the organization in which the decision is made on the effectiveness of the decision support system. Even if the decision maker acts alone, he has to take into consideration the organizational context. It is thus not only necessary to recognize the existence of key elements of the organization in a DSS framework, but to identify them also. These elements include the people involved, the history dependence (i.e., tradition, commitments), the degree of dependence on other decisions problems (see for example, Ginzberg, 1980). How do these organizational factors increase or reduce the functional behavior of the decision maker(s)? How can one control possible dysfunctionality induced by the organizations, and enforce appropriate correction mechanisms?

R9. *JUSTIFY:* Studies have shown that the pre-decision and post-decision phases are sometimes more crucial than the decision phase itself. A classical example of this is the elimination of a decision due to the inability of the decision maker to persuade other organizational forces. The issue here is how much one should pay attention to the justification levels. Do the efforts of persuading others about a course of action help the decision-makers' sharpen their own conviction of the line of action taken?

R10. *ORGANIZE:* Unlike the literature in systems analysis and design that deals extensively with organizational aspects of elaborating and implementing data processing systems (e.g., chief programmer team, steering committee), the issues of organizing are often missing in the literature of building decision support systems. What is the optimal division of labor between human experts and computerized decision support? If more than one human expert or consultant is involved, what is the ideal form of team work?

12.4 IMPLICATIONS OF THE MODEL FOR GDSS DESIGN

The E-R model views organizational decision making as a set of loosely coupled activities associated with different entities. As discussed, the activities must be considered as loosely coupled because they are rarely applied simultaneously nor with the same intensity. These observations have a number of implications for DSS design.

A hypothetical organizational DSS would have to take into account *all* elements of the E-R model. At any time, users must be able to keep all elements in mind; otherwise, the effectiveness of decision making would be impeded. For example, the organization must constantly watch the ACCESSIBLE REAL WORLD to identify new opportunities (ALTERNATIVES for action) and changing perceptions (PERCEIVE). Similarly, ignoring the ORGANIZATIONAL CONTEXT may lead to decisions that cannot be appropriately implemented.

However, building an integrated GDSS covering all aspects of organization decision making appears currently infeasible, given the complexity, the costs implicated, and eventually the unwillingness of involved users to use and share the system in its totality. Fortunately, the relative importance of these elements — i.e., the major focus of attention — varies according to the specific problems to be solved at a particular point in time. Tailored DSS packages are often better suited to these specific problems than general-purpose tools that attempt to address all aspects in a superficial fashion.

In order to avoid a multiplicity of incompatible specific DSS, the organizational GDSS should have a *modularized* architecture that contains a set of specific DSS capable of covering all entities and relationships of the model when coupled together. This approach provides specific tools for each individual problem while ensuring some coherence of the decision processes. The modular structure permits each of the organizational needs to be supported progressively and independently by computerized decision aids. Specific or application-dependent DSS can be built to support each organizational entity and its associated relationships.

The next issue is how this coherence can be ensured. First, the integration of specific DSS necessitates a *process perspective* provided by the relationships of the model, which in turn are guided by the MCDM processes. In other words, if the current focus of attention is on DSS tools for a particular activity (say, JUDGE), easy access must also be provided to DSS for neighboring activities (e.g., PERCEIVE, ANALYZE); the sequence of accessible DSS may be determined, e.g., by some stochastic models of typical decision procedures.

Second, from a software viewpoint, we advocate a *loose coupling strategy* of specific DSS. Loose coupling implies that each specific DSS is self-contained but equipped with gateways to interact with other specific DSS within the same GDSS. Gateways are used to share data and models, and to adjust different user interfaces such that some consistency is offered to the users. Besides avoiding the complexity of a more integrated approach, loose-coupling also simplifies system maintenance in that new DSS can constantly be added to replace outdated ones. Furthermore, development costs can be reduced by incorporating purchased DSS into the GDSS architecture.

12.5 EXTENDING A GDSS FOR ORGANIZATIONAL DECISION SUPPORT: THE CASE OF Co-oP

The E-R model can also be used to demonstrate that DSS currently used in organizations support only some of the major elements of the organizational decision-making processes. Existing DSS take into account only some of the described entities and relationships. Figure 12.5 suggests how some decision making models fits in with the E-R framework. For instance, the simulation of the Garbage Can Model would only help understand organizational phenomena described in entities E3, E4 and the relationship R4. Similarly, distributed data bases and recent attempts to establish micro-mainframe links would support only E1, E2 and R1.

Figure 15.5 also suggests that among the decision tools listed, MCDM-based group DSS seem to cover the largest number of elements of the E-R model. Therefore, it would make a great deal of sense to assume that MCDM-based group DSS is a prime candidate to be extended to support organization decision making. The question is then how can a MCDM-based such as Co-oP can be extended to fit the E-R model?

12.5.1 Co-oP as a Special Case of the E-R Model

As described in Chapter 8, Co-oP is a network of microcomputer-based process-driven DSS for cooperative multiple criteria group decision support system. Each decision maker has his own individual DSS whose model base offers, among other tools, multiple criteria decision methods (MCDM). The group DSS contains a set of techniques of aggregation of preferences and negotiation support algorithms that can be used in conjunction with individual MCDM.

DECISION MAKING METHODOLOGY	CORRESPONDING ELEMENTS IN THE E-R MODEL	SOME EXAMPLES OF DSS
FORECASTING /SIMULATION	E3,R4,E4	Garbage-Can (Cohen, March, and Olsen 1972, Carley, 1984, Anderson and Fisher, 1984) Stochastic modeling (Bui, Sivasankaran, Eoyang, 1986)
OPTIMIZATION TECHNIQUES	E3,R4,E4,R5,E5	Industrial Dynamics (Forrester, 1961)
MC-DSS	E3,R4,E4,R5,E5,R3,E7	AHP (Saaty, 1980)
GDSS	E3,R4,E4,R5,E5,R3,E7, R7,R10	Co-oP

Figure 12.5. Decision Methods and the E-R Model

In chapter 8, we discussed six main group decision processes in Co-oP. These processes include (i) group norm definition, (ii) group problem definition, (iii) individual and group prioritization of objectives or criteria, (iv) individual evaluation of alternatives, (v) group aggregation of preferences, and (iv) consensus seeking. We now analyze each of these steps in terms of the E-R model.

The group problem and group norm definitions consist of requesting the decision makers to collectively identify and define an organizational decision problem (DECISION MAKERS, DECISION ALTERNATIVES, EVALUATION CRITERIA, and to a degree, ORGANIZATIONAL CONTEXT). For instance, Co-oP allows definition of organizational distribution of power using weighing scheme, and setting of deadlines to submit opinions. The decision makers also have to agree upon the way the group DSS handles data transfers, interactive conversation, utilization of electronic mail, and the type(s) of group decision techniques (NEGOTIATE and IMPOSE).

The Co-oP process of prioritization of evaluation criteria corresponds to the JUDGE relationship. This process can be accomplished by requesting organizational members to assign weights to the criteria directly, or by using a hierarchical prioritization scheme. The Co-oP collective prioritization process can be performed in pooled mode (i.e., all group members enter 'collectively' a priority vector), in sequential mode (i.e., group members assign priority to a subset of criteria according to their expertise), or in aggregation mode (i.e., each member performs individual weighing first; then individual priorities are aggregated using a pre-determined computation rule).

The ANALYZE relation is embedded in the fourth Co-oP process. This process allows the organizational decision makers to individually evaluate alternatives using their preferred or familiar MCDM. Its acts as a single user multiple criteria DSS with data communications support.

The computation of group results, as a function of ACT, can be accomplished by using appropriate aggregation of preferences techniques stored in the Co-oP Model Base. If unanimity is not obtained, a consensus-seeking algorithm (Bui, 1985a) can be evoked in the sixth and last phase (NEGOTIATE). If impasse still prevails, decision makers can attempt to revise their problem representations by going back to any of the previous processes.

In order to monitor loosely-coupled activities, the decision processes are controlled by a communications component (Bui and Jarke, 1986). This GDSS component can be viewed as a meta-system that performs three roles: (i) coordinator (i.e., to provide maximum support for information exchange); (ii) detective (i.e., to enforce communication protocols derived from ORGANIZATIONAL CONTEXT), and (iii) inventor (i.e., to search for data compatibility for group algorithms and sort data for diffusion).

12.5.2 Extension Required for Organizational Decision Support

Expanding Co-oP for organizational support requires a double operation: (i) enhancements of existing functional capabilities, and (ii) insertion of additional organizational decision support tools. In other words, ACCESSIBLE REAL WORLD, KNOWN WORLD, DECISION ANALYSTS, ACQUIRE, GENERATE, PERCEIVE, and IMPOSE should be added or expanded to grasp better the decision structure of the organization.

Concretely, the following considerations should be added into the basic decision activities currently supported by Co-oP:

(1) *Organizational Context Monitoring:* In an ORGANIZA-TIONAL CONTEXT, the detective role of the communications component should include regulations and historical practices of

the organization (IMPOSE). The JUSTIFY relationship is already supported by the current Co-oP version in that graphics tools can be used to illustrate the decision process, but it could be enhanced by explicitly referring to organizational norms and practices.

(2) *Re-apportionment of tasks:* The division of tasks between DECISION MAKERS and DECISION ANALYSTS should be explicitly defined in the Problem definition module. Unlike the decision maker, a decision analyst assesses a problem but may not participate in the choice process. This distinction generally holds for the prioritization of evaluation criteria, the selection of alternatives, group aggregation of preferences, and consensus seeking.

(3) *Integration of the Acquisition activity:* The alternatives as well as their characteristics are assumed to be known prior to the use of the current version of Co-oP. The KNOWN WORLD concept can be realized by coupling Co-oP with a data base management system (DBMS). The acquisition process would require the development of a complete data-centered approach to information gathering. This process could be achieved by sorting data given certain evaluation criteria, by distributing data to functional centers (e.g., Jarke, 1982), or defining some collectively acceptable norms to coordinate different user views of databases (Jarke et al., 1986).

(4) *Integration of the Generation activity:* In Co-oP, the process of generating new problem perspectives could be achieved by two distinct operations. First, given the acquisition capability (i.e., ACQUIRE), expansion of new alternatives can be obtained by withdrawing norms previously defined in the Group norm

monitor and the problem definition. Second, the search for new decision problems could be derived by the learning process.

SUMMARY

This chapter presented a framework for building organizational GDSS. Based on the concept of multiple criteria decision making, an Entity-Relationship model was proposed as a framework for designing DSS for organizations. The model contains eight entities and ten relationships that embed major factors affecting organizational decision making. The purpose of this model is to (i) decompose the organizational decision-making processes, (ii) classify current DSS and their limitations, and to (iii) identify design opportunities for DSS for organizations. In particular, this chapter advocated that DSS in organizations should be group-oriented, modularized, process-oriented and composed of loosely-coupled special-purpose DSS.

Using Co-oP as an example, this chapter also attempted to show that a multiple criteria group DSS architecture can be expanded to organizational DSS. The most urgent additions appear to be the integration of environmental factors and organizational contexts, the generation of new decision spaces, and the understanding of the roles of different types of actors.

13. CONCLUSIONS

The purpose of this research was to elaborate a methodology for group decision support systems, and to design a DSS for cooperative multiple criteria group decision making.

13.1 SUMMARY OF FINDINGS

As a result of the analysis, design, implementation and testing of Co-oP — a DSS for cooperative multiple criteria group decision making — the major findings of this research are enumerated below:

13.1.1 An Architecture for Group Decision Support Systems

From a methodological point of view, this research argued for a distributed, loosely-coupled, and process-driven group decision support system (GDSS). The rationale of this proposition can be summarized as follows:

First, given the unpredictable nature of group decision problems, group decision processes were shown to be the only elements in the GDSS that are (i) stable enough to fit into most collective problems; (ii) reasonably structurable and therefore implementable, and (iii) sufficiently controllable to warrant appropriate use (Chapter 4 and 5).

Second, given the diversity of decision approaches adopted by decision makers, this research suggested the design of two independent but interrelated content-driven decision tools. The first group of decision models are individual-oriented to provide personalized support to group members. These decision techniques are stored in individual model bases. The second group of decision models deals with techniques of aggregation of preferences and algorithms for consensus seeking. They are stored in a group model base (Chapter 8).

The decision techniques in the GDSS are loosely coupled via a structured sequence of group decision processes. The latter includes (i) group norm definition, (ii) group problem definition, (iii) individual and group prioritization of evaluation of objectives or criteria, (iv) individual evaluation of alternatives, (v) group aggregation of preferences, and (iv) consensus seeking. This structured sequence of processes is further intertwined with (preset) electronic and format-free communications (e.g., electronic mail, online discussion) (Chapter 6, 7 and 8).

Such a loosely-coupled GDSS architecture would provide autonomy and flexibility for individual decision making, and homogeneity and simplicity for group problem solving (Chapter 6).

13.1.2 Communications Issues in GDSS

In the context of a distributed group decision situation, this research supported conceptualization of an information exchange as being format-transparent, adaptable to the circumstances and requirements of a specific group. It advocated the creation of a communications component as a fourth component of the DSS architecture. Such a component would play three roles: (i) coordinator (i.e., to provide maximum support for information exchange), (ii) detective (i.e., to enforce communication protocols), and (iii) inventor (i.e., to search for data compatibility for group algorithms and sort data for diffusion) (Chapter 7).

10.1.3 Consensus Seeking Algorithm in GDSS

This research also presented an consensus-seeking algorithm. The latter is based on a three-part concept: expansion, contraction, and intersection. The proposed algorithm could be viewed as an extension of techniques of aggregation of preferences. More importantly, it could be used as an early detector that identifies boundaries between conflict resolution and conflict dissolution.

13.1.4 Conceptualization of a Unified MCDM-GDSS

This study discussed a framework for a unified MCDM model case. The interfacing and combined use of various multiple criteria decision methods would help a MCDM-based GDSS support a wide range of decision situations, attenuate the difficulty of information search, and allow division of decision making tasks (Chapter 2 and 5).

More important, the suggested multiple criteria group DSS is extensible to organizational DSS. The addition of processes that help introduce environmental factors and organizational contexts, generate new decision spaces, and take into the decision problem a larger population of actors, would constitute a step towards organizational DSS (Chapter 3 and 12).

13.1.5 Evaluation Framework for GDSS

This research also overviews current propositions to evaluate GDSS and proposes a contingency model of effective GDSS use as a function of one of the most critical organizational parameters — problem types. The purpose of the model it to help identify prime organizational problem solving opportunities for GDSS use. We believe that this contingency model can be served as a framework for empirically evaluating GDSS effectiveness (Chapter 9). An early experimental evaluation was conducted (Chapter 10)

13.1.6 Non-cooperation

Assuming that a basic approach to effective non-cooperative problem solving is to restore the trust and confidence of the parties, a fundamental mission of a GDSS is to reduce resistance to use the system as a channel or medium for resolving a collective problem. Under certain circumstances, GDSS could be used as a appropriate means to handle non-cooperative problems (Chapter 11). They constitute a promising adjunct to the exclusive use of human mediation in orchestrating a constructive group decision-making process. Benefits derived from using GDSS may include improvement of communication, understanding, and ultimately, problem settlement.

13.1.7 Towards Organizational DSS

Based on the experience gained with the use of Co-oP and the development of a Entity-relationship model of organizational decision making, this research formulated some design considerations for building DSS to support organizational decision making. The most urgent additions appear to be the integration of environmental factors and organizational contexts, the generation of new decision spaces, and the understanding of the roles of different types of actors. This research advocated that DSS in organizations should be group-oriented, modularized, process-oriented and composed of loosely-coupled special-purpose DSS.

13.2 SUGGESTIONS FOR FUTURE RESEARCH

Given the scope of this research, there are a number of research issues that remained untreated in this study. Among these, one could identify at least three issues that would deserve immediate follow-up.

13.2.1 Extensions of the Current Version of Co-oP

The implemented version of Co-oP has suggested that there is at least one solution to each of the design considerations discussed in this work. Yet, alternative solutions to the design issues should be explored. Also, Co-oP could be expanded to attain its full strength. First, additional individual MCDM could be integrated in the Co-oP model component. Second, a more flexible data manager would make it easier for the GDSS to handle manipulation of decision data. Such extensions would transform Co-oP into a generalized multiple criteria group DSS.

13.2.2 Development of Distributed Knowledge Bases

This research issued some guidelines for integrating distributed knowledge bases in GDSS (Section 5.6). The implementation of such knowledge bases would drastically improve the supporting role of GDSS given the complexity of group decision situations. It would also allow GDSS to evolve with its users and their decisional context, and thus, reduce the unpredictability of the nature of the group problem.

13.2.3 Experimental Investigation of the Effects of GDSS on Group Decision Making

Last but not least, as the review of the interdisciplinary literature suggested (Chapter 3), there have been more opinions than facts in the analysis and design of group decision support systems. More extensive and careful experimental studies on implemented and operating GDSS — such as Co-oP conducted in this research — would definitely yield additional guidelines in the effective design of group decision support systems.

BIBLIOGRAPHY

Ackoff, R.L. (1978), *The Art of Problem Solving*, Wiley and Sons.

Aldrich, H. and D. Herker (1977), "Boundary Spanning Roles and Organization Structure", *Academy of Management Review*, 2, 217-230.

Allen S. (1970), "Corporate-Divisional Relationships in Highly Diversified Firms", *Studies in Organizational Design*, Lorsch and Lawrence (Eds), Irwin, Homewood, Illinois, 16-35.

Allison, G.T. (1970), *Essence of Decision*, Little Brown, Boston.

Alter, S. (1980), *Decision Support Systems: Current Practices and Continuing Challenges, Reading*, Mass., Addison-Wesley.

Anderson, P.A., and G.W. Fisher (1984), "A Monte Carlo Model of Garbage Can Decision Processes," *Stanford University-Naval Postgraduate School Joint Workshop on Decision Making in Military Organizations*, Monterey, CA., Jan 26-28.

Applegate, L., t. Chen, B. Konsynski and J. Nunamaker, Jr. (1987), "Knowledge Management in Planning", *Journal of Management Information Systems*, 3, 4, Spring, 20-38.

Ariav G. and M. Ginzberg (1985), "Understanding DSS -- A Systemic View of Decision Support", *Communications of the ACM*.

Armstrong, R.D., W.D. Cook and L.M. Seiford (1982), "Priority Ranking and Consensus Formation: The Case of Ties", *Management Science*, 28, 6, 638-645.

Arrow, K.J. (1963), *Social Choice and Individual Values*, 2nd ed., New York, Wiley.

Ashby, W.R. (1952), *Design for a Brain*, John Wiley, New York.

Asch S. (1951), "Effects of Group Pressure on the Modification and Distortion of Judgments", *Group, Leadership and Men*, Guetzkow (Ed), Pittsburgh, Carnegie Press, 174-183.

Bales, R.F. and F.L. Strodtbeck (1951), "Phases in Group Problem Solving", *Journal of Abnormal Social and Psychology*, 46, 485-495.

Bales, R.F. (1955), "How People Interact in Conferences", *Scientific American*, March, 3-7.

Bancilhon, F, Kim, W and Korth, H.F. (1985), "A Model of CAD Transactions", *Proceedings 11th International Conference on Very Large Data Bases*, Stockholm, 25-33.

Barber, G.R. (1984), "Trends in Artificial Intelligence: Research and Applications", *Organisation for Economic Co-operation and Development,* Paris, ICCP(84)2.

Barclay, S. and C.R. Peterson (1976), "Multi-attribute Utility Models for Negotiations", Working Paper, Virginia, Decisions and Designs, Inc.

Bartunek, J.M. and A. Benton, and C. Keys (1977), "Third Party Intervention and the Bargaining Behavior of Group Representatives", *Journal of Conflict Resolution,* 19, 532-557.

Bass B.M. (1983), *Organizational Decision Making,* Richard Irwin, New York.

Beer S. (1975), *A Platform for Change,* Chichester, England, John Wiley and Sons.

Benbassat I. and Y. Wand, (1983), "A Structured Approach to Designing Human/Computer Interface", *International Journal of Man Machine Studies.*

Benbassat I. and A. S. Dexter (1984), "An Experimental Investigation of Color-Enhanced and Graphical Information Systems under Varying Levels of Time Pressure", working paper, Faculty of Commerce, University of British Columbia, forthcoming *Management Science.*

Bennett, J. (ed) (1983), *Building Decision Support Systems,* Addision Wesley Reading, Mass.

Bereanu, B. (1976), "Large Group Decision Making with Multiple Criteria", in Thiriez and Zionts (eds.), *Multiple Criteria Decision Making,* Springer Verlag, 87-101.

Bernard, D. (1979), "Management Issues in Cooperative Computing", *Computing Surveys,* 11, 1, 3-17.

Black, D. (1958), *The Theory of Committees and Elections,* Cambridge University Press, Cambridge.

Blake, R.R. (1979) "Intergroup problem-solving in organizations: From theory to practice," in *The social psychology of intergroup relations,* Austin and Worchel (ed.), Monterey, Ca., Brooks, Cole.

Blanning, R. W. (1982), "Data Management and Model Management: A Relational Synthesis", *International Journal of Policy Analysis and Information Systems,* 6, 4, 313-323.

Blanning, R.W. (1983), "Issues in the Design of Relational Model Management Systems", *AFIPS Conference Proceedings: 1983 National Computer Conference,* 395-401.

Blau, J.H. (1972), "A Direct Proof of Arrow's Theorem", *Econometrica,* 40, 1, 61-67.

Bogart, K.P. (1973), "Preferences Structures I: Distances Between Transitive Preference Relations", *Journal of Mathematical Sociology*, Vol. 3, 49-67.

Bogart, K.P. (1975), "Preference Structures II: Distances Between Asymmetric Relations", *Journal of Applied Mathematics*, 29, 2, 254-262.

Boje, D. and K. Murninghan (1982), "Group Confidence Pressures in Iterative Decisions", *Management Science*, 1987-1196.

Bonczek, R. H., C. Holsapple, and A. Whinston (1979), "Computer-based Support of Organizational Decision Making", *Decision Sciences*, 268-291.

Bonczek, R.H., C.W. Holsapple and A.B. Whinston (1980), "A Generalized Decision Support System using Predicate Calculus Network Data Base Management", *Operations Research*, 29, 2, 263-281.

Bonczek, R.H., W.W. Holsapple and A.B. Whinston (1981), *Foundations of Decision Support Systems*, New York, Academic Press.

Borda, J.C. (1781), "Memoire sur les Elections au Scrutin", *Histoire de l'Academie Royale de Science*, Paris.

Borland International (1985), *Sidekick: The Desktop Organizer just a Keystroke away*, Borland International, Scotts Valley, California.

Bowman, V.J. and C.S. Colantoni (1973), "Majority Rule under Transitivity Constraints", *Management Science*, 19, 9, 1029-1041.

Bui, X.T. (1980), *Essais d'optimisation dimensionnelle et structurelle de l'entreprise*, University of Fribourg Press, 1980.

Bui, X.T. (1982), *Executive Planning with BASIC*, Berkeley, Sybex.

Bui, X.T. (1984), "Building Effective Multiple Criteria Decision Making: A Decision Support System Approach", *Systems, Objectives, Solutions*, 4, 1, 3-16.

Bui, X.T. (1985), "NAI -- A Consensus Seeking Algorithm for Group Decision Support Systems", *Proceedings of the 1985 IEEE International Conference on Systems, Man and Cybernetics*, Tucson, Arizona.

Bui, X.T. and M. Jarke (1984), "A Decision Support System for Cooperative Multiple Criteria Group Decision Making", *Proceedings of the 6th International Conference on Information Systems*, Tucson, Arizona, 101-113.

Bui, X.T. and M. Jarke (1985), "Communications Requirements for Group Decision Support Systems", *Proceedings of the 19th Hawaii International Conference on System Sciences*, Honolulu, Hawaii, January, 1986, Journal of MIS, Spring 1986.

Bui, X.T. and M. Jarke (1986), "Communications Design for Co-oP: A Group Decision Support System", *ACM Transactions on Office Information Systems*, April 1986.

Bui, X.T. and M. Jarke (1987), "Design Considerations for GDSS in Organizations", working paper, Naval Postgraduate School, Monterey, California.

Bui, X.T., M. Jarke and M.F. Shakun (1987), "Non-Cooperation in GDSS", working paper, Naval Postgraduate School, Monterey, California.

Bui, X.T. and M.F. Shakun (1987), "NAI: The Negotiable Alternatives Identifier", working paper, Naval Postgraduate School, Monterey, California.

Bui, X. T. and J. Pasquier (1984), "A DSS for Selecting Micro-Computers", working paper, University of Fribourg.

Bui, X.T. and T. Sivasankaran (1987), "Integrating Modular Design with Adaptive Design in DSS Prototyping: An Archepelagian Approach", *Procedings of the 20th Annual Hawaii International conference of System Sciences*, 736-745.

Bui, X.T., T. Sivasankaran, Y. Fiyol and M. Woodberry (1987), "Identifying Organizational Opportunities for GDSS Use: Some Experimental Evidence", *DSS-87 Transactions*, San Francisco, 68-75.

Bui, X.T. and T.R. Sivisansaran and C. Eoyang (1987), "A Cybernetic Model for Organizational Decision Making", working paper, Naval Postgraduate School, Monterey, California.

Carley, K. (1984), "Garbage Can Efficiency - A Simulation", *Stanford University-Naval Postgraduate School Joint Workshop on Decision Making in Military Organizations*, Monterey, CA., Jan 26-28.

Carlson, E.D. and J.A. Sutton (1974), "A Case Study of Non-Programmer Interactive Problem Solving", *IBM Research Report RJ 1382*, San Jose, California.

Cartwright, D. and A. Zander (Eds.) (1968), *Group Dynamics*, 3rd edition, Evanston, Illinois, Row, Peterson.

Case, J.H. (1979), *Economics and the Competitive Process*, New York, New York University Press.

Chamberlain, N. and J. Kuhn (1965), *Collective Bargaining*, New-York, Mc-GrawHill.

Chatterjee K and J. Ulvila (1982), "Bargaining with Shared Information", *Decision Sciences*, 380-480.

Chen, P. (1976), *The Entity-Relationship Model, ACM Transactions on Databases*, 1, 9-36.

Chesnut, R. and J. Jacoby (1982), "Behavioral Process Research: Concept and Application in Consumer Decision Making", Ungson and Braunstein (Eds), *Decision Making*, Boston, Mass., Kent Publishing Co.

Christie, B. (1981), *Face to File Communication*, New York, Wiley.

Cohen M.D., J. March, and J. Olsen (1972), "A Garbage Can Model of Organizational Choice", *Administrative Sciences Quarterly*, 17, 1, 1-23.

Connolly, T. (1977), "Information Processing and Decision Making in Organizations", Staw and Salancik (eds.), *New Directions in Organizational Behavior*, Chicago, St. Clair Press.

Connolly, T.(1980), "The Decision Competence Paradox", Huseman (Ed.), *Proceedings of the Academy of Management*, Detroit.

Cook, R. and K. Hammond (1982), "Interpersonal Learning and Interpersonal Conflict Reduction in Decision Making Groups" in R.A. Guzzo (ed.), *Improving Group Decision Making*, New York, Academic Press, 13-72.

Cook, W.D. and L.M. Seiford (1978), "Priority Ranking and Consensus Formation", *Management Science*, 24, 16, 1721-1732.

Cook, W.D. and L.M. Seiford (1982), "On the Borda-Kendall Consensus Method for Priority Ranking Problems", *Management Science*, 28, 6, 621-637.

Crama, Y. and P. Hansen (1983), "An Introduction to the ELECTRE Research Program", in Beckmann and Krelle (Eds), *Essays and Surveys on Multiple Criteria Decision Making*, New York, Springer-Verlag.

Crawford, V.P. (1985), "Dynamic games and dynamic contract theory", *Journal of Conflict Resolution*, 29, 2, pp. 195-224.

Crozier, M. (1964), *The Bureaucratic Phenomenon*, Chicago, The University of Chicago Press.

Cummings, L., G. Huber, and E. Arendt (1974), "Effect of Size and Spatial Arrangements on Group Decision Making", *Academy of Management Journal*, 460-475.

Cyert, R.M and J.G. March (1963), *A Behavioral Theory of the Firm*, Englewood Cliffs, New Jersey, Prentice Hall.

Davis, J.H. (1973), "Group Decision and Social Interaction: A Theory of Social Decision Schemes", *Psychological Review*, 97-125.

Davis, R. (1979), "Interactive Transfer of Expertise: Acquisition for New Inference Rule", *Artificial Intelligence*, 12, 121-157.

Davis, R. (1982), "Expert Systems: Where are we? And where do we go from here?", *A.I. Memo No. 665*, MIT Artifical Intelligence Laboratory.

Davis, R. and J. King (1976), "An Overview of Production Systems", Elcock and Michie (eds), *Machine Intelligence*, New York, Wiley, 300-332.

Davis, R. and R.G. Smith (1983), "Negotiation as a Metaphor for Distributed Problem Solving", *Artificial Intelligence*, 20, 63-109.

Davis, O.A, DeGroot, M.H. and Hinich, M.J. (1972), "Social Preference Orderings and Majority Rule", *Econometrica*, 40, 1, 147-157.

Dearborn, D. and H. Simon (1958), "Selective Perception: a Note on the Departmental Identification of Executives", *Sociometry*, 21, 140-144.

Delbecq, A.L. (1968), "The World within the 'Span of Control': Managerial Behavior in Groups of Varied Size", *Business Horizons*, August.

DeSanctis G. and F. Gallupe (1985), "Group Decision Support Systems: A new Frontier", *Database*, 2, 3-11.

DeSanctis G. and F. Gallupe (1987), "A Foundation for the Study of Group Decision Support Systems", *Management Science*, Vol. 33, No. 5, May, pp. 589-609.

Deutsch, M. (1973), *The Resolution of Conflict*, New Haven Connecticut, Yale University Press.

Deutsch, M. and R.H. Krauss (1962), "Studies of Interpersonal Bargaining", *Journal of Conflict Resolution*, 52-76.

Dickson, G. (1983), "Requisite Functions for a Management Support Facility" in J. Sol (ed.), *Processes and Tools for Decision Support*, Amsterdam, North Holland.

Dolk, D.R. (1983), "A Knowledge-Based Model Management System for Mathematical Programming", Working Paper, Naval Postgraduate School, Monterey, California.

Donovan, J. (1976), "Data Base System Approach to Management Decision Support", *Transactions on Database Systems*, 1, 4, 344-369.

Dorris, J.W., G.C. Gentry and H.H. Kelly (1972), "The Effects on Bargaining of Problem Difficulty, Mode of Interaction and Initial Orientation", Working Paper, University of Massachusetts.

Douglas, A. (1962), *Industrial Peace Making*, New York, Columbia Press.

Downs, A. (1966), *Inside Bureaucracy*, Boston, Little, Brown.

Duda, R.O. and J.G. Gaschnig (1981), "Knowledge-based Expert Systems Come of Age", *Byte*, 6, 9, 238-281.

Dutton, W., J. Fulk and C. Steinfield (1982), "Utilizing of Video Conferencing", *Telecommunications Policy*, September, pp. 164-178.

Dyer, J.S. (1972), "Interactive Goal Programming", *Management Science*, 19, 1, 62-70.

Dyer, J.S. and Wehrung (1973), "A Time Sharing Computer Program for the Solution of the Multiple Criteria Problem", *Management Science*, 19, 12, 1379-1383.

EDP Analyzer (1984), "Get ready to offer group services", *EDP Analyzer*, 22, 10.

Edelstein, M. and M. Melnyk (1982), "Decision Support Systems for Fleet Planning" in Ginzberg, Reitman, Stohr (eds), *Decision Support Systems*, Amsterdam, North-Holland, 121-132.

Edgeworth, F.W. (1881), *Mathematical Psychics: An Essay on the Application of Mathematics to the Moral Sciences*, London, Kegan Paul and Co.

Edwards, W. (1961), "Behavioral Decision Theory", *Annual Review of Psychology*, 12, 473-498.

Edwards, W. (1977), "Use of Multiattribute Utility Measurement for Social Decision Making" in Bell, Keeney and Raiffa (eds.), *Conflicting Objectives in Decisions*, New York, Wiley, also in *IEEE Transactions on Systems*, Man Cybernetics, SMC-7, pp. 326-340.

Einhorn, H.J. (1978), "Learning from Experience and Suboptimal Rules in Decision Making", Wallsten (Ed.), *Cognitive Processes in Choice and Decision Behavior*, Hillsdale, New Jersey, Erlbaum.

Eiseman, J. (1977), "A Third Party Consultation Model for Resolving Recurring Conflicts Collaboratively", *Journal of Applied Behavioral Science*, 303-314.

Elam, J.J., J.C. Henderson and L.W. Miller (1980), "Model Management Systems: An Approach to Decision Support in Complex Organizations", *Proceedings First International Conference on Information Systems*.

Evans, G.W. (1984), "An Overview of Techniques for solving Multiobjective Mathematical Programs", *Management Science*, 30, 11, 1268-1282.

Farquhar, P.H. (1977), "A Survey of Multiattribute Utility Theory and Applications" in Starr and Zeleny (eds), *Multiple Criteria Decision Making*, Amsterdam, North-Holland.

Farquhar, P.H. (1984), "Utility Assessment Methods", *Management Science*, 30, 11, 1283-1300.

Fedorowicz, J., N. Soderstrom and J. Clark (1986) , "DSS Usage Patterns and the Decision Making Process: A Research Methodology", *DSS Transactions*, Washington D.C., 89-95.

Feldman, D (1984), "The Development and Enforcement of Group Norms", *Academy of Management Review*, 47-53.

Ferguson, J. and Johansen (eds) (1975), *Teleconference on Integrated Data Bases in Postsecondary Education*, Indianapolis, Indiana, and Institute for the Future, Lilly Endowment, Inc.

Fick, G. and R.H. Sprague (Eds.) (1981), *Decision Support Systems: Issues and Challenges*, Oxford, Pergamon Press.

Fischoff, B, P. Slovic, P, and S Lichtenstein (1980), "Knowing what you want: Measuring Labile Values", Wallsten (Ed.), *Cognitive Processes in Choice and Decision Behavior*, Hillsdate, New Jersey, Erlbaum.

Fishburn, P.C. (1971), "A Comparative Analysis of Group Decision Methods", *Behavioral Science*, 16, 538-544.

Fishburn, P.C. (1978), "A Survey of Multi-Attribute/ Multi- criterion Evaluation Theories" in Zionts (ed), *Multiple Criteria Problem Solving*, New York, Springer-Verlag.

Fishburn, P.C. and W. Gehrlein (1977), "Towards a Theory of Elections Probabilistic Preferences", *Econometrica*, 45, 1907-1923.

Fishburn, P.C. (1984), "Multiattribute Nonlinear Utility Theory", *Management Science*, November, 1301-1322.

Fisher, R. (1978), *International Mediation: A Working Guide*, New York International Peace Academy.

Fogg, R.W. (1985), "Dealing with Conflict: A Repertoire of Creative, Peaceful Approaches", *Journal of Conflict Resolution*, 29, 2, 330-358.

Forrester J.W. (1961), *Industrial Dynamics*, New York, John Wiley.

Froman, L.A., Jr. and M. Cohen (1970), "Compromise and Logroll: Comparing the Efficiency of Two Bargaining Processes", *Behavioral Science*, 15, 180-183.

Gardner, W.R. (1970), "Good Patterns have few Alternatives", *American Scientist*, 58, 34-42.

Galbraith, J. (1977), *Organization Design*, New York, Addison-Wesley.

Galbraith, J.K. (1967), *The New Industrial State*, London, Hamish Hamilton.

Galbraith, J.K. (1973), "Power and the Useful Economist", Presidential Address in the American Economic Association, *American Economic Review*.

Gallupe, B. (1986), "Experimental Research into GDSS: Practical Issues and Problems", *Proceedings of the 19th HICSS*, Honolulu, 524-533.

Geoffrion, A.M., J.S. Dyer and A. Feinberg (1972), "An Interactive Approach for Multi-criterion Optimization with an Application to the Operation of an Academic Department", *Management Science*, 14, 357-358.

Gessford, J.E. (1980), *Modern Information Systems, Designed for Decision Support*, Reading, Mass., Addison-Wesley.

Ginzberg, M.J. (1980), "The Impact of Organizational Characteristics on MIS Design and Implementation", *ORSA/TIMS Joint National Meeting*, Colorado Spring, November, 10-12.

Ginzberg M.J. and E.A. Stohr (1982), "Decision Support Systems: Issues and Perspectives" in Ginzberg M.J., W. Reitman and E.A. Stohr (eds), *Decision Support Systems*, Amsterdam, North-Holland, 9-31.

Gorry G.A. and M.S. Scott-Morton (1971), "A Framework for MIS", *Sloan Management Review*, 13, 1, 55-70.

Gray P. (1981), "The SMU Decision Room Project", *Transactions on the First International Conference on Decision Support Systems*, DSS-81, Atlanta, 122-129.

Gray P. (1983), "Initial Observations from the Decision Room Project", *Transactions of the 3rd International Conference on Decision Support Systems*, Boston, Massachusetts.

Gray P. (1987), "Panel on Frontiers in DSS:L Group Decision Support and Cooperative Work", *DSS-87 Transactions,* San Francisco, 159.

Hackathorn R. and P. Keen (1981), "Organizational Strategies for Personal Computing in Decision Support Systems", *MIS Quarterly*, 5, 3., 21-27.

Hackman, J.R. and R. Kaplan (1974), "Interventions into Group Process: An Approach to Improving the Effectiveness of Groups", *Decision Sciences*, 5, 459-480.

Hall, W.A. and Y.Y. Haimes (1976), "The Surrogate Worth Trade-Off Method with Multiple Decision Makers" in Zeleny, *Multiple Criteria Decision Making*, Kyoto 1975, New York, Springer-Verlag.

Hammond, D.R. (1965), "Mew Directions in Research on Conflict Resolution", *Journal of Social Issues*, 11, 44-46.

Hammond, D.R. and L. Alderman (1976), "Science, Values and Human Judgment", *Science*, 194, 389-396.

Harrison, E.F. (1975), *The Managerial Decision-Making Process*, Boston, Massachussetts, Houghton Mifflin.

Harsanyi, J.C. (1955), "Cardinal Welfare and Individualistic Ethics and Interpersonal Comparisons of Utility", *Journal of Political Economy*, 63, 309-321.

Hart, S., M. Boroush, G. Enk and W. Hornick (1985), "Managing Complexity Through Consensus Mapping: Technology for the Structuring of Group Decisions", *Academy of Management Review*, 10, 3, 587-600.

HEAT (1983), *Commands and Controls Effectiveness Experiments: Comparing Geographic and Functional C-2 Organization*, Defense Communications Agency, U.S. Naval Postgraduate School, Monterey, California.

Heidel, K.J. and L. Duckstein (1983), "Extension of ELECTRE Technique to Group Decision Making: An application to Fuel Emergency Control", working paper, TIMS/ORSA Joint National Meeting, Chicago, April 1983.

Henderson, J.C and P. Nutt, "The Influence of Decision Style on Decision Making Behavior", *Management Science*, 26, 371-386.

Hills, R.W. and T. Mahoney (1978), "University Budgets and Organizational Decision Making", *Administrative Science Quarterly*, 23, 464-465.

Hiltz, S.R. and M. Turoff (1978), *The Network Nation, Human Communication via Computer*, Reading, Mass., Addison-Wesley.

Hiltz, S.R., C. Johnson, C. Aronovitch, and M. Turoff (1980), "Face-to-Face vs. Computerized Conferences: A Controlled Experiment", Report 12, New Jersey Institute of Technology, Computerized Conferencing and Communications Center.

Hoffman, L.R. (1965), "Group Problem Solving" in L. Berkowitz (Ed.), *Advances in Experimental Social Psychology*, 2, New York, Academic Press, 99-132.

Hoffman, P.J. (1960), "The Parmorphic Representation of Clinical Judgment", *Pschological Bulletin*, 57, 2, 116-131.

Holloman, C.R. and H. Hendrick, "Adequacy of Group Decisions as a Function of the Decision Making Process", *Academy of Management Journal*, 15, 176-184.

Holloway, C.A. and P.E. Mantey (1975), "An Interactive Procedure for the School Boundary Problem with Declining Enrollments", *Operations Research*, 23, 2, 191-206.

Huber G. (1982), "Organizational Information Systems: Determinants of their Performance and Behavior", *Management Science*, 28, 6, 138-155.

Huber, G. (1982), "Group Decision Support Systems as Aids in the Use of Structured Group Management Techniques", *DSS-82 Conference Proceedings*, 96-103.

Huber, G.P. (1983), "Cognitive Styles as a Basis for MIS and DSS Design: Much Ado About Nothing?", *Management Science*, 27, 5, pp. 567-585.

Huber G. (1984), "Issues in the Design of Group Decision Support Systems, *MIS Quarterly*, 8, 3, 195-204.

Hwang, C.L. and A.S.M. Masud (1979), *Multiple Objective Decision Making -- Methods and Applications*, New York, Springer-Verlag.

Ilich, J. (1980), *Power Negotiating*, Reading, Mass., Addison Wesley.

Inada, K. (1969), "The Simple Majority Rule", *Econometrica*, 37, 3, 490-506.

ISO (1982), *Data Processing — Open Systems Interconnection Reference Model, International Organization for Standardization*, ISO / TC97 / SC16 - N890.

Jacquet-Lagreze, E. and J. Siskos (1982), "Assessing a Set of Additive Utility Functions for Multiple Criteria Decision Making — The UTA Method", *European Journal of Operational Research*, 10, 2, 151-164.

Jacquet-Lagreze, E. and M. F.Shakun (1984), "Decision Support Systems for Semi-Structured Buying Decisions", NYU-GBA Working Paper.

Jacoby, J. (1977), "Information Load and Decision Quality: some Issues", *Journal of Marketing Research*, 14, 569-573.

Jantsch, E. (1967), *Technological Forecasting in Perspective*, Organization for Economic Cooperation and Development, Paris.

Jarke, M. (1982), "Developing Decision Support Systems: a Container Management Example", *International Journal of Policy Analysis and Information Systems*, 6, 4, 351-372.

Jarke, M., T. Jelassi and M. Shakun (1987), "MEDIATOR: Towards a Negotiation Support System", to appear in M.F. Shakun, *Evolutionary Systems Design — Policy Making Under Complexity*, Holden Day.

Jarke, M, T. Bui and M. Jelassi (1985), "Micro-mainframe DSS for remote multiple user decision making", in Jarke (ed), *Managers, Micros, and Mainframes*, John Wiley and Sons, New York.

Jarke, M. (1986), "Knowledge Sharing and Negotiation Support in Multiple person Decision Support Systems", *Decision Support Systems*, 2, 1, pp. 93-102.

Johansen, R., J. Vallee and K. Collins (1978), "Learning the Limits of Teleconferencing: Design of a Teleconferencing Tutorial" in M.C. Elton, W. Lucas and D. Conrath (Eds.), *Evaluating new Telecommunication Systems*, New York, Plenum.

Johansen, R., J. Vallee and K. Spangler (1979), *Electronic Meetings: Technical Alternatives and Social Choices*, Reading, Mass., Addison-Wesley.

Johansen, R. and C. Bullen (1984), "What to expect from Teleconferencing", *Harvard Business Review*, March-April, 164-174.

Jones, A.J. (1980), *Game Theory, Mathematical Models of Conflict*, New York, Wiley.

Kahan, J.P. and A. Rapaport (1984), *Theories of Coalition Formation*, Lawrence Erlbaum Associates, Inc..

Kalai, E. and M. Smorodinsky (1975), "Other Solutions to Nash Bargaining Problem", *Econometrica*, 43, 513-518.

Kanter, J. (1977), *Management-oriented Management Information Systems*, Englewood Cliffs, New Jersey, Prentice-Hall.

Keen, P.G.W. (1977), "The Involving Concept of Optimality", *TIMS Studies in the Management Sciences*, 6, 31-57.

Keen, P.G.W. (1981), "Value Analysis: Justifying Decision Support Systems", *MIS Quarterly*, March, 1-15.

Keen, P.G.W. and M. Scott-Morton (1978), *Decision Support Systems: An Organizational Perspective*, Reading, Mass, Addision-Wesley.

Keeny, R.L. (1976), "A Group Preference Axiomatization with Cardinal Utility", *Management Science*, 23, 2, 140-145.

Keeny, R.L. and C.W. Kirkwood (1975), "Group Decision Making using Cardinal Social Welfare Functions", *Management Science*, 22, 4, 430-437.

Keeny, R.L., R.H. Mohring, H. Otway, F.J. Radermacher and M.M. Richter (Eds.), "Multi-Attribute Decision Making Via O.R.-Based Expert Systems", Conference Report, University of Passau, April 20-27, 1986.

Kelley, H. and J. Thibaut (1969), "Group Problem Solving" in G. Lindsey and E. Aronson (Eds), *The Handbook of Social Psychology*, 2nd edition, Reading, Mass., Addison-Wesley.

Kemeny, J.G. and L.J. Snell (1962), "Preference Ranking: An Axiomatic Approach", in Ginn, *Mathematical Models in the Social Sciences*, New York, 9-23.

Kendall, M. (1962), *Rank Correlation Methods*, 3rd ed., New York, Hafner.

Klahold, P., Schlageter, G., Unland, R. and Wilkes, W. (1985), "A Transaction Model Supporting Complex Applications in Integrated Information Systems", *Proceedings ACM/SIGMOD Conference*, Austin, Tx., 388-401.

Kleinmutz, B. (1975), "The Computer as Clinician", *American Psychologist*, 30, 379-387.

Kochan, T.A., and Jick, T. (1978), "The Public Sector Mediation Process: A Theory and Empirical Examination", *Journal of Conflict Resolution*, 22, 209-240.

Kolasa, B.J. (1975), "Social Influence of Groups" in R. Steers and L. Porter (Eds.), *Motivation and Work Behavior*, New York, Mc-Grawhill.

Kolb D.A., I.M. Rubin and J. McIntyre (1984), *Organizational Psychology*, 4th edition, New Jersey, Prentice Hall.

Konsynski, B., and D. Dolk (1982), "Knowledge Abstractions and Model Management", *Proceedings of DSS-82*, 187-202.

Korhonen, P., J. Wallenius, and S. Zionts (1980), "Some Thoughts on Solving the Multiple Decision Maker/Multiple Criteria Decision Problem and an Approach", Working Paper, No. 414, State University of New York at Buffalo.

Krauss, R.M. and M. Deutsch (1966), "Communication in Interpersonal Bargaining", *Journal of Personality and Social Psychology*, 9., 15-20.

Kressel, K. (1981), "Kissinger in the Middle East: An Exploratory Analysis of Role Strain in International Negotiation", in *Dynamics of Third Party Intervention: Kissinger in the Middle East*, J.Z. Rubin (ed.), New York, Praeger.

Kull, F.J. (1982), "Group Decisions: Can Computers Help?", *Computer Decisions*, 14, 5, 70-82.

Levy, M.A. (1985), "Mediation of Prisoners'Dilemma Conflicts and the Importance of the Cooperation Threshold", *Journal of Conflict Resolution*, 29, 4, December, 581-603.

Licker P. and R. Thompson (1985), "Consulting Systems: Group Decision Support by one Person", *Proceedings of the 18th Annual Hawaii International Conference on System Sciences*, Hawaii, 466-475.

Likert, R. (1967), *The Human Organization*, New York, McGraw-Hill.

Lindblom, C. (1956), "The Science of Muddling Through", *Public Administration Review*, 19, 59-88.

Lindstone, H.A. and M. Turoff(1975), *The Delphi Method:Techniques and Applications,* Addison-Wesley, Reading, Mass..

Litterer, J. (1966), "Conflict in Organizations: a Re–Examination", *Academy of Management Journal*, 178-186.

Little J.C. (1970), "Models and Managers: The concept of a Decision Calculus", *Management Science*, 16, 8, 466-485.

Lochard, J. and J. Siskos, "La gestion des risques environ- mentaux d'origine industrielle", C.E.P.N., Centre d'etude sur l'Evaluation de la Protection dans le domaine nucleaire, 92260 Fontenay-aux-Roses, France.

Luce, R.D. and H. Raiffa (1957), *Games and Decisions,* New York, Wiley.

McCosh, A.M., and M.S. Scott Morton (1978), *Management Decision Support Systems,* New York, John Wiley and Sons.

March, J.G. (1962), "The Business Firm as a Political Coalition", *The Journal of Politics*, 24, pp. 662-678.

March, J. (1978), "Bounded Rationality, Ambiguity, and the Engineering of Choice", *Bell Journal of Economics*, 9, 587-608.

March, J. (1981), "Decisions in Organizations and Theory of Choice", Ven de Ven and Joyce (Eds.), *Assessing Organizational Design and Performance*, New York, Wiley.

March, J., and J.P. Olsen (1976), *Ambiguity and Choice in Organizations*, Bergen:Universitetsforlage.

March, J. and Z. Shapira (1982), "Behavioral Decision Theory and Oganizational Decision Theory", Ungson and Braunstein, *Decision Making*, Boston, Mass., Kent Publishing Co., 92-107.

March, J. and H. Simon (1958), *Organizations*, New York, Wiley.

Marschak, J. (1955), "Elements for a Theory of Teams", *Management Science*, 1, 127-137.

Martin, J. (1981), *Computer Networks and Distributed Processing*, Englewood Cliffs, New Jersey, Prentice Hall.

Mason, R.O. and I. Mitroff (1973), "A Program for Research on Management Information Systems", *Management Science*, 19, 4, 475-487.

McCrimmon, K.R. (1977), "An Overview of Multiple Objective Decision Making" in Cochrane and Zeleny (eds), *Multiple Criteria Decision Making*, University of South Carolina Press, South Carolina.

Miles, R.E. and C.Snow (1978), *Organizational Strategy, Structure and Process*, New York, McGraw-Hill.

Miller, G.A. (1956), "The Magical Number Seven, Plus or Minus Two: Some Limits on our Capacity for Processing Information", *Management Science*, 81-97.

Mintzberg, H. (1971), "Managerial Work Analysis from Observations", *Management Science*, 18, 2, 97-110.

Mintzberg, H. (1973), *The Nature of Managerial Work*, New York, Harper and Row.

Mintzberg, H.E. (1973), "Strategy Making in Three Modes", *California Management Review*, 16, 2, 44-53.

Mintzberg, H., D. Raisinghani, and A. Theoret (1976), "The Structure of 'Unstructured' Decision Processes", *Administrative Sciences Quarterly*, 21, 2, 246-275.

Mitroff I. and M. Turoff (1975), "Philosophical and Methodological Foundations of Delphi", in *The Delphi Method: Techniques and Applications*, Reading, Mass., Addison-Wesley.

Mock, M.K. and L. Pondy (1977), "The Structure of Chaos: Organized Anarchy as a Response to Ambiguity", *Administrative Sciences Quarterly*, 22, 351.

More J.H. and M.G. Chang (1980), "Design of Decision Support Systems", *Data Base*, 12, 1, 2, 8-14.

Morley, I.E. and G.M. Stevenson (1970), "Formality in Experi- mental Negotiations: A Validation Study", *British Journal of Psychology*, 1.

Morley, L. and J. Stephensen (1977), *The Social Psychology of Bargaining*, London, Allen and Unwin.

Morse, J.N. (1980), "Reducing the Size of the Non-dominated Set: Pruning by Clustering", in Zeleny, *Computers and Operations Research: Special Issue on Mathematical Programming with Multiple Objectives*, 7, 1-2, 55-66.

Moscarola, J. and B. Roy (1977), "Procedure Automatique d'examen de dossiers fondee sur une segmentation trichotomique en presence de criteres multiples", *RAIRO Operations Research*, 11, 2, 145-173.

Moskowitz, H., J. Wallenius, P. Korhonen and S. Zionts (1981), "A Man-Machine Interactive Approach to Collective Bargaining", Working Paper, No. 521, School of Management, SUNY, Buffalo.

Mueller, D.C. (1976), "Public Choice: A Survey", *Journal of Economic Literature*, 14, 2, 395-433.

Murrel, S. (1983), "Computer Communication System affects Group Decision Making", *Proceedings of the Conference on Computer and Human Interaction*, Boston, Mass., 63-67.

Nash, J.F. (1950),"The Bargaining Problem", *Econometrica*, 18, 155-162.

National Bureau of Standards (1982) , "The Selection of Local Area Computer Networks", *Computer Science and Technology*, U.S. Department of Commerce, November 1982.

Naumann, J., and M. Jenkins (1982), "Prototyping: The New Paradigm for Systems Development", *MIS Quarterly*, September, 29-44.

Nguyen, H.D. (1980), "Selection des actions financieres, La methode ELECTRE III", *Memoire de licence*, Institute for Economic and Social Sciences, University of Fribourg.

Nicholson, W. (1978), *Microeconomic Theory: Basic Principles and Extensions*, Hinsdale, Illinois, The Dryden Press.

Nitzan, S. and J. Paroush (1983), "Small Panels of Experts in Dichotomous ChoiceSituations", *Decision Sciences*, 14, 314- 325.

Olson, M.H. (1983) "Remote Office Work: Changing Patterns in Space and Time", *Communications of the ACM*, Vol. 26, No. 3.

O'Reilly, C. (1982), "Variations in Decision Makers' Use of Information Sources: The Impact of Quality and Accessibility of Information", *Academy of Management Journal*, 4, 756-771.

O'Reilly, C. and H. Anderson (1979), "Organizational Communication and Decision Making: Laboratory Results versus Actual Organizational Setting, *Proceedings of the 24th International Meeting of the Institute of Management Sciences*, Honolulu.

Padgett, J. (1980), "Managing Garbage Can Hierarchies", *Administrative Science Quarterly*, 583-604.

Pareto, V. (1896), *Course d'economie politique*, Lausanne, Rouge.

Pasquier, J., T. Bui, M. Vieli and L. Wuillemin (1979), "Choix d'un projet d'investissement a Bulle pour l'entreprise DSA-SFSA", Working Paper 79, University of Fribourg, Fribourg.

Pasquier et al. (1981), "Analyse multicritere de fusion d'entreprise" in E. Borsberg (ed), *Strategies et diversification d'entreprise*, Lausanne.

Perrow, C. (1970), *Organizational Analysis: A Sociological View*, Belmont, California, Wadsworth Publishing Co.

Perrow, C. (1972), *Complex Organizations: A Critical Essay*, 2nd edition, Glenview, Illinois, Scott, Foresman.

Perrow, C. (1979), *Organizational Analysis: A Sociological View*, Wadsworth Publ. Co., Belmont, CA.

Pfeffer, J. (1981), "Organizations and Organization Theory" in Lindzey and Aronson (des), *Handbook of Social Psychology*, 3rd edition, Reading, Mass., Addison-Wesley.

Phillips, L.D. (1980), *Organization Structure and Decision Technology*, Acta Psychologica, 45, 247-264.

Plott, C.R. (1976), "Axiomatic Social Choice Theory: An Overview and Interpretation", *American Journal of Political Science*, 20, 3, 511-596.

Plott., C.R. and M.E. Levine (1978), "A Model of Agenda Influence on Committee Decisions", *American Economic Review*, 68, 146-160.

Popper, K. (1959), *The Logic of Scientific Discovery*, Hutchinson, London.

Pruitt, D.G. (1981), *Negotiation Behavior*, New York, Academic Press, 1981.

Puzman J. and R. Porizek (1980), *Communication Control in Computer Networks*, John Wiley and Sons, Chicester.

Pye, R., B.C. Champness, H. Collins and S. Connell (1973), "The Description and Classification of Meetings", Unpublished Communications Studies Group paper, N.o P/73160/PY.

Quinn, J.B. (1980), *Strategy for Change*, Homewood for Change, Richard Irwin.

Quirk, J.P. and R. Saposnik (1962), "Adminissibility and Measurable Utility Functions", *Review of Economic Studies*, Vol. 29, 140-146.

Radner, R. and M. Rothschild (1975), "On the Allocation of Effort", *Journal of Economic Theory,* 10, pp. 358-376.

Rados, D.L. (1972), "Selection and Evaluation of Alternatives in Repetitive Decision Making", *Administrative Science Quarterly,* 17, 196-296.

Rao, A.G. and M.F. Shakun (1974), "A Normative Model for Negotiations, *Management Science,* 20, 10.

Reitman, W. (1982), "Applying Artificial Intelligence to Decision Support", in M. Ginzberg, W. Reitman, E. A. Stohr (eds), *Decision Support Systems,* Amsterdam, North-Holland, 155-174.

Rockart, J.F. (1979), "Chief Executives Define their Own Data Needs", *Harvard Business Review,* 72, 81-93.

Rockart, J.F. (1982), "The Changing Role of the Information System Executive: A Critical Success Factors Perspective", *Sloan Mangement Review,* 24, 1.

Rouse W.B. (1981), "Human-Computer Interaction in the Control of Dynamic Systems", *Computing Surveys,* 23, 1, 71-99.

Roy, B. (1968), "Classement et choix en presence de points de vue multiples (la methode ELECTRE)", *R.I.R.O.,* 2, 57-75.

Roy, B. (1971), "Problems and Methods with Multiple Objective Functions, *Mathematical Programming,* 2, 239-266.

Roy, B. and P. Bertier (1973), "La methode ELECTRE II, une application au media-planning", in M. Ross, (ed), OR 72 (Dublin 1972), Amsterdam, North-Holland, 291-302.

Roy, B. (1976), "A Conceptual Framework for a Normative Theory of Decision Aids", *Management Science.*

Roy, B. (1978), "ELECTRE III: un algorithme de rangement fonde sur une presentation floue des preferences en presence de criteres multiples", Cahiers du Centre d'Etudes de Recherche Operationnelle, 20, Paris, 3-24.

Rubin, J.R. and B.R. Brown (1975), *The Social Psychology of Bargaining and Negotiation,* New York, Academic Press.

Rubin, J.R. (1980), "Experimental Research on Third Party Intervention: Towards some Generalizations", *Psychological Bulletin,* 379-390.

Rubin, J.R. (1981), *Dynamics of Third Party Intervention,* New York, Praeger.

Russo, J. (1974), "More Information is Better: a Reevaluation of Jacoby, Speller, and Kohn", *Journal of Consumer Research,* 1, 68-72.

Saaty, T. (1980), *The Analytic Hierarchy Process: Planning, Priority, Allocation*, New York, Mac-GrawHill.

Sabrosky, A., J.C. Thompson, and K.A. McPherson (1982), "Organized Anarchies: Military Bureaucracy in the 1980's", *Journal of Applied Behavioral Science*, 18, 2, pp. 137-153.

Sanders, G.L., J. Courtney, S. Loy (1984), "The impact of DSS on Organizational Communications", *Information and Management*, 7, 2, 141-148.

Savage, L.J. (1954), *The Foundations of Statistics*, John Wiley, New York.

Schneiderman, B. (1986), *Designing the User Interface*, Addison-Wesley.

Seo, F. (1984), "Multiatrribute Utility Analysis and Collective Choice, A Methodological Review", *Proceedings of the VIth International Conference on Multiple Criteria Decision Making*, Case Institute of Technology, Cleveland, June 1984.

Shakun, M.F. (1981a), "Formalizing Conflict Resolution in Policy Making", *International Journal of General Systems*, 7, 3, 207-215.

Shakun, M.F. (1981b), "Policy Making and Meaning as Design of Purposeful Systems", *International Journal of General Systems*, 7, 3, 207-215.

Shakun, M.F. (1987), "Decision Support Systems for Negotiations, in M.F. Shakun (ed.), *Evolutionary Systems Design: Policy Making under Complexity*, Holden Day, San Francisco.

Shenoy, P. (1980), "On Committee Decision Making: A Game Theoretical Approach, *Management Science*, 26, 4, 387-399.

Shepard, R. (1964), "On Subjectively Optimum Selections among Multi-attribute Alternatives", Shelly and Bryan (Eds.), *Human Jugments and Optimality*, New York, Wiley.

Sherif, M. and C. Sherif (1969), *Social Psychology*, New York, Harper and Row.

Shneiderman, B. (1980), *Software Psychology: Human Factors in Computer and Information Systems*, Cambridge, Mass., Winthrop.

Short, J. (1974), "Effect of Medium of Communication on Experimental Negotiation", *Human Relations*, 27, 225-334.

Short, J., E. Williams and B. Christie (1976), *The Social Psychology of Communications*, London, Wiley.

Shubik, M. (1962), *Strategy and Market Structure*, New York, John Wiley.

Shwartz, S.P. (1984), "Natural Language Processing in the Communications World", in Reitman (ed), *Artificial Intelligence Applications for Business,* Norwood, New Jersey, Ablex Publishing Corporation.

Simkin, W.E. (1971), *Mediation and the Dynamics of Collective Bargaining,* Washington D.C., Bureau of National Affairs.

Simon, H.A. (1957), *Models of Man,* John Wiley, New York.

Simon, H. (1965), *The Shape of Automation for Men and Management,* New York, Harper and Row.

Simon, H. (1967), "The Compensation of Executives", *Sociometry,* March.

Simon, H.A. (1969), *The Science of the Artificial,* MIT Press, Cambridge, MA.

Simon, H. (1973), "Applying Information Technology to Organization Design", *Public Administration Review,* 33, 3, 268-278.

Spelt, P.F. (1977), "Evaluation of a Continuing Computer", *Conference on Simulation, Behavior Research Methods and Instrumentation,* Spring.

Sprague, R. and E. Carlson (1982), *Building Effective Decision Support Systems,* Englewood Cliffs, Prentice Hall.

Starr, M.K. and M. Zeleny (1977) "MCDM — State and Future of the Art, *TIMS Studies in the Management Sciences,* 6, 5-29.

Steeb, R. and S.C. Johnston (1981), "A Computer-based Interactive System for Group Decision Making", *IEEE Transactions on Systems, Man, and Cybernetics,* SMC-11, 8, 544-552.

Stefik M., G. Foster, D. Borrow, K. Kahn, S.Lanning and L. Suchman (1987), "Beyond the Chalkboard: Computer Support for Collaboration and Problem Solving in Meetings", *Communications of the ACM,* Vol. 30, No. 1, 32-47.

Steinbruner, J.D. (1974), *The Cybernetic Theory of Decision,* Princeton University Press, Princeton, NJ.

Steuer, R.E. (1979), "Goal Programming Sensitivity Analysis Using Interval Penalty Weights", *Mathematical Programming,* 17, 1, 16-31.

Steuer, R.E. and A.T. Schuler (1978), "An Interactive Multiple Objective Linear Programming Approach to a Problem in Forest Management", *Operations Research,* 26, 2, 254-269.

Stevens, C.M. (1963), *Strategy amd Collective Bargaining Negotiations,* New York, McGraw-Hill.

Stigler, J.E. (1961), "The Economics of Information", *Journal of Political Economy*, 213-225.

Stohr, E.A. (1981), "DSS for Cooperative Decision-Making", *Proceedings NATO Conference on Data Base and Decision Support Systems*, Amsterdam, North-Holland.

Stohr, E.A. and N.H. White (1982), "User Interfaces for Decision Support Systems: An Overview", *International Journal of Policy Analysis and Information Systems*, 6.

Stohr, E.A. and N.H. White (1983), "Languages for Decision Support Systems: An Overview", *Management and Office Information Systems*, S.K.Chang (ed), New York, Plenum Press.

Suchan J., T. Bui and D. Dolk (1987), "GDSS Effectiveness: Identifying Organizational Opportunities", *Proceedings of the 1987 Hawaii International Conference of System Sciences*, Kailua-Kona, Hawaii.

Szilagyi, A. and M. Wallace (1980), *Organizational Behavior and Performance*, Santa Monica, Goodyear Publishing Company.

Tanenbaum (1981), *Computer Networks*, New York, Prentice Hall.

Thibaut, J.W. and H. Kelley (1959), *The Social Psychology of Groups*, New York, John Wiley.

Thierauf, R.J. (1982), *Decision Support Systems for Effective Planning and Control*, Englewood Cliffs, New Jersey, Prentice-Hall.

Thiriez, H. and D. Houri (1975), "Multi-person Multi-criteria Decision Making: A sample Approach", in Thiriez and Zionts, *Proceedings of Multiple Criteria Decision Making*, Springer Verlag.

Thompson, J.D (1967), *Organizations in Action*, New York, McGraw-Hill.

Trauth, E., S. Kwan and S. Barber (1984), "Channel Selection and Effective Communication for Managerial Decision making", *ACM Transactions on Office Information Systems*, 2, 2, 123-140.

Tucker, A.W., et al. (eds) (1950, 1953, 1957, 1959, and 1964), *Contributions to the Theory of Games*, Vol. I, II, III, IV; and *Advances in Game Theory*, Annals of Mathematics Studies, Nos. 24, 28, 39, 40, and 52, Princeton, Princeton University Press.

Turoff, M. and S. Hiltz (1982), "Computer Support for Group Individual Decisions", *IEEE Transactions on Communications* COM-30, 1, 82-90.

Tversky, A., and D. Kahneman (1985), "Judgments Under Uncertainty: Heuristics and Biases," *Science*, 1, 1124-1131.

Ungson G.R. and D. N. Braunstein (1982), *Decision Making, A Interdisciplinary Inquiry*, Kent Publishing Company, Bostor Massachusetts.

Van Aken (1982), *On the Understanding of Complex Organizatior* Netherlands.

Van de Ven, A.H. (1974), *Group Decision Making and Effectivenes* Graduate School of Business, Kent State University, 93-105.

Van de Ven, A.H. and A.L. Delbecq (1974), "The Effectiveness • Nominal, Delphi and Interacting Group Decision Making Processes *Academy of Management*, 17, 4, 605-621.

Van Gundy, A.B. (1981), *Techniques of Structured Problem Solvin* New York, Von Nostrand Reinhold.

Vogel, D., J. Nunamaker, L. Applegate, and B. Konsynski (1987 "Group Decision Support Systems: Determinants for Success", *DS 87 Transactions*, San Francisco, 118-128.

von Neumann J. and O. Morgenstern (1953), *Theory of Games a Economic Behavior*, 3rd ed., Princeton, New Jersey, Princet University Press.

von Winterfeldt, D. and W. Edwards (1986), *Decision Analysis a Behavioral Research*, Cambridge University Press, New York.

Vroom, V.H. and P.Yetton (1973), *Leadership and Decision Makir* Pittsburgh, University of Pittsburgh Press.

Vroom, V.H. and A.D. Jago (1974), "Decision Making as a Soc Process: Normative Descriptive Models of Leader Behavio *Decision Sciences*, 5.

Wall, J. (1981), "Mediation: An Analysis, Review and Propos Research", *Journal of Conflict Resolution*, March.

Walton, R. (1969), *Interpersonal Peacemaking: Confrontations and Th Party Consultation*, Reading, Mass., Addison Wesley.

Walton, R. and R. McKensie (1965), *A Behavioral Theory of Lat Negotiations*, New York.

Warr, P. (1973), *Psychology and Collective Bargaining*, London.

Weick, K.E. (1979), *The Social Psychology of Organizing*, 2nd • Reading, Mass., Addison-Wesley.

Wendell, R.E. (1979), "Multiple Objective Mathematical Programm with Respect to Multiple Decision-Makers", *Operations Research*, 5, 1100-1111.

Wichman, H. (1970), "Effects of Isolation and Communication on Cooperation in a Two Person Game", *Journal of Pers. Soc. Psychology*, 16, 114-120.

Wiener, N. (1948), *Cybernetics*, John Wiley, New York.

Wierzbicki, A. P. (1983), "Critical Essay on the Methodology of Multi-Objective analysis", *Regional Science and Urban Economics*, 13, 5-29.

Williams, E. (1978), "Telecommunications: Social and Psychological Factors", *Journal of Communication*, 125-131.

Williamson, O.E. (1975), *Markets and Hierarchies*, Free Press, New York.

Winograd, T. and Flores, F. (1986), *Understanding Computers and Cognition: A New Foundation for Design*, Norwood, N.J., Ablex.

Young, H.P. (1974), "An Axiomatization of Borda's Rule", *Journal of Economic Theory*, 9, 1, 43-52.

Young, H.P. (1977), "Extending Condorcet's Rule", *Journal of Economic Theory*, 16, 2, 335-353.

Yu, P.L. (1973), "A Class of Solutions for Group Decision Problems", *Management Science*, 19, 8., 936-946.

Yu, P.L. (1981), "Behavior Bases and Habitual Domains of Human Decision/Common Wisdom", *International Journal of Systems, Measurement and Decisions*, 1, 39-62.

Yu, P.L. (1984), "Behavior Mechanism in Decision Making", Working Paper, University of Kansas, Lawrence.

Zartman, I.W. (ed) (1978), *The Negotiation Process*, Beverly Hill, Ca., Sage.

Zionts, S. and J. Wallenius (1976), "An Interactive Programming Method for Solving the Multiple Criteria Problem", *Management Science*, 22, 6, 652-663.

Zeleny, M. (1982), *Multiple Objective Decision Making*, Mass., Addison-Wesley.

Zmud, R. (1979), "Individual Differences and MIS Success: A Review of the Empirical Literature", *Management Science*, 960-979.

INDEX

Vol. 245: H.F. de Groote, Lectures on the Complexity of Bilinear Problems. V, 135 pages. 1987.

Vol. 246: Graph-Theoretic Concepts in Computer Science. Proceedings, 1986. Edited by G. Tinhofer and G. Schmidt. VII, 307 pages. 1987.

Vol. 247: STACS 87. Proceedings, 1987. Edited by F.J. Brandenburg, G. Vidal-Naquet and M. Wirsing. X, 484 pages. 1987.

Vol. 248: Networking in Open Systems. Proceedings, 1986. Edited by G. Müller and R.P. Blanc. VI, 441 pages. 1987.

Vol. 249: TAPSOFT '87. Volume 1. Proceedings, 1987. Edited by H. Ehrig, R. Kowalski, G. Levi and U. Montanari. XIV, 289 pages. 1987.

Vol. 250: TAPSOFT '87. Volume 2. Proceedings, 1987. Edited by H. Ehrig, R. Kowalski, G. Levi and U. Montanari. XIV, 336 pages. 1987.

Vol. 251: V. Akman, Unobstructed Shortest Paths in Polyhedral Environments. VII, 103 pages. 1987.

Vol. 252: VDM '87. VDM – A Formal Method at Work. Proceedings, 1987. Edited by D. Bjørner, C.B. Jones, M. Mac an Airchinnigh and E.J. Neuhold. IX, 422 pages. 1987.

Vol. 253: J.D. Becker, I. Eisele (Eds.), WOPPLOT 86. Parallel Processing: Logic, Organization, and Technology. Proceedings, 1986. V, 226 pages. 1987.

Vol. 254: Petri Nets: Central Models and Their Properties. Advances in Petri Nets 1986, Part I. Proceedings, 1986. Edited by W. Brauer, W. Reisig and G. Rozenberg. X, 480 pages. 1987.

Vol. 255: Petri Nets: Applications and Relationships to Other Models of Concurrency. Advances in Petri Nets 1986, Part II. Proceedings, 1986. Edited by W. Brauer, W. Reisig and G. Rozenberg. X, 516 pages. 1987.

Vol. 256: Rewriting Techniques and Applications. Proceedings, 1987. Edited by P. Lescanne. VI, 285 pages. 1987.

Vol. 257: Database Machine Performance: Modeling Methodologies and Evaluation Strategies. Edited by F. Cesarini and S. Salza. X, 250 pages. 1987.

Vol. 258: PARLE, Parallel Architectures and Languages Europe. Volume I. Proceedings, 1987. Edited by J.W. de Bakker, A.J. Nijman and P.C. Treleaven. XII, 480 pages. 1987.

Vol. 259: PARLE, Parallel Architectures and Languages Europe. Volume II. Proceedings, 1987. Edited by J.W. de Bakker, A.J. Nijman and P.C. Treleaven. XII, 464 pages. 1987.

Vol. 260: D.C. Luckham, F.W. von Henke, B. Krieg-Brückner, O. Owe, ANNA, A Language for Annotating Ada Programs. V, 143 pages. 1987.

Vol. 261: J. Ch. Freytag, Translating Relational Queries into Iterative Programs. XI, 131 pages. 1987.

Vol. 262: A. Burns, A.M. Lister, A.J. Wellings, A Review of Ada Tasking. VIII, 141 pages. 1987.

Vol. 263: A.M. Odlyzko (Ed.), Advances in Cryptology – CRYPTO '86. Proceedings. XI, 489 pages. 1987.

Vol. 264: E. Wada (Ed.), Logic Programming '86. Proceedings, 1986. VI, 179 pages. 1987.

Vol. 265: K.P. Jantke (Ed.), Analogical and Inductive Inference. Proceedings, 1986. VI, 227 pages. 1987.

Vol. 266: G. Rozenberg (Ed.), Advances in Petri Nets 1987. VI, 451 pages. 1987.

Vol. 267: Th. Ottmann (Ed.), Automata, Languages and Programming. Proceedings, 1987. X, 565 pages. 1987.

Vol. 268: P.M. Pardalos, J.B. Rosen, Constrained Global Optimization: Algorithms and Applications. VII, 143 pages. 1987.

Vol. 269: A. Albrecht, H. Jung, K. Mehlhorn (Eds.), Parallel Algorithms and Architectures. Proceedings, 1987. Approx. 205 pages. 1987.

Vol. 270: E. Börger (Ed.), Computation Theory and Logic. IX, 442 pages. 1987.

Vol. 271: D. Snyers, A. Thayse, From Logic Design to Logic Programming. IV, 125 pages. 1987.

Vol. 272: P. Treleaven, M. Vanneschi (Eds.), Future Parallel Computers. Proceedings, 1986. V, 492 pages. 1987.

Vol. 273: J.S. Royer, A Connotational Theory of Program Structure. V, 186 pages. 1987.

Vol. 274: G. Kahn (Ed.), Functional Programming Languages and Computer Architecture. Proceedings. VI, 470 pages. 1987.

Vol. 275: A.N. Habermann, U. Montanari (Eds.), System Development and Ada. Proceedings, 1986. V, 305 pages. 1987.

Vol. 276: J. Bézivin, J.-M. Hullot, P. Cointe, H. Lieberman (Eds.), ECOOP '87. European Conference on Object-Oriented Programming. Proceedings. VI, 273 pages. 1987.

Vol. 277: B. Benninghofen, S. Kemmerich, M.M. Richter, Systems of Reductions. X, 265 pages. 1987.

Vol. 278: L. Budach, R.G. Bukharajev, O.B. Lupanov (Eds.), Fundamentals of Computation Theory. Proceedings, 1987. XIV, 505 pages. 1987.

Vol. 279: J.H. Fasel, R.M. Keller (Eds.), Graph Reduction. Proceedings, 1986. XVI, 450 pages. 1987.

Vol. 280: M. Venturini Zilli (Ed.), Mathematical Models for the Semantics of Parallelism. Proceedings, 1986. V, 231 pages. 1987.

Vol. 281: A. Kelemenová, J. Kelemen (Eds.), Trends, Techniques, and Problems in Theoretical Computer Science. Proceedings, 1986. VI, 213 pages. 1987.

Vol. 282: P. Gorny, M.J. Tauber (Eds.), Visualization in Programming. Proceedings, 1986. VII, 210 pages. 1987.

Vol. 283: D.H. Pitt, A. Poigné, D.E. Rydeheard (Eds.), Category Theory and Computer Science. Proceedings, 1987. V, 300 pages. 1987.

Vol. 284: A. Kündig, R.E. Bührer, J. Dähler (Eds.), Embedded Systems. Proceedings, 1986. V, 207 pages. 1987.

Vol. 285: C. Delgado Kloos, Semantics of Digital Circuits. IX, 124 pages. 1987.

Vol. 286: B. Bouchon, R.R. Yager (Eds.), Uncertainty in Knowledge-Based Systems. Proceedings, 1986. VII, 405 pages. 1987.

Vol. 287: K.V. Nori (Ed.), Foundations of Software Technology and Theoretical Computer Science. Proceedings, 1987. IX, 540 pages. 1987.

Vol. 288: A. Blikle, MetaSoft Primer. XIII, 140 pages. 1987.

Vol. 289: H.K. Nichols, D. Simpson (Eds.), ESEC '87. 1st European Software Engineering Conference. Proceedings, 1987. XII, 404 pages. 1987.

Vol. 290: T.X. Bui, Co-oP A Group Decision Support System for Cooperative Multiple Criteria Group Decision Making. XIII, 250 pages. 1987.